TER~~

Someone to Love Us²

The Shocking True Story of Two Brothers
Fostered into Brutality and Neglect

HarperElement
An Imprint of HarperCollins*Publishers*
77–85 Fulham Palace Road,
Hammersmith, London W6 8JB

www.harpercollins.co.uk

and *HarperElement* are trademarks
of HarperCollins*Publishers* Ltd

First published by HarperElement 2010

1 3 5 7 9 10 8 6 4 2

© Terence O'Neill 2010

Terence O'Neill asserts the moral right to
be identified as the author of this work

A catalogue record of this book is
available from the British Library

ISBN 978-0-00-735018-6

Printed and bound in Great Britain by
Clays Ltd, St Ives plc

Mixed Sources

Product group from well-managed
forests and other controlled sources
www.fsc.org Cert no. SW-COC-001806
© 1996 Forest Stewardship Council

FSC is a non-profit international organization established to promote the
responsible management of the world's forests. Products carrying the FSC
label are independently certified to assure consumers that they come
from forests that are managed to meet the social, economic and
ecological needs of present and future generations.

Find out more about HarperCollins and the environment at
www.harpercollins.co.uk/green

Dedicated to the memory of my dear brother
"DENNY"
(3 March 1932 – 9 January 1945)

Acknowledgements

My sincere thanks to my editor Gill Paul for her sensitive and dedicated professionalism, and for her friendship. I am most grateful to Charissa Warme and Carole Tonkinson of HarperCollins for finding my story on Authonomy and deciding it was worthy of publication. My thanks to Kate Latham, also of HarperCollins, for her kindness and guidance.

My gratitude to my wife Pat for all her support and help, my two daughters Maria and Julie for their patience and understanding over the years, and my dear granddaughter Melissa who helped with the typing and also helped me to master the computer. My thanks to my dear grandchildren Laura and Adam for their encouragement and help over recent years.

I am most grateful to my old friends, especially Denis, Gladys, Tony and John, for their belief that my story would eventually be published.

Foreword

'Hello, boys,' Miss Edwards said, giving us a bright smile. 'I'm here from Newport Council to see how you're getting on. Does life on a farm suit you?'

'It's OK,' I mumbled, but Dennis just stared at the ground.

'Do you like your school?'

'It's fine,' I said.

Mrs Gough, our foster mother, gave a big, false kind of a smile. 'Go on, Terence. Tell Miss Edwards what you've been doing at school.' She continued, without giving me a chance: 'They've been making Christmas decorations and a nativity scene and he's been learning all the old carols too. I keep hearing him singing them round the place.'

I didn't think she'd ever once heard me singing in the six months I'd been at Bank Farm but I knew better than to contradict her.

'Are you all right, Dennis?' Miss Edwards asked him, and he nodded without looking at her. 'You look awfully pale. Are you feeling all right?'

Mrs Gough answered for him: 'He's had a nasty cough but he's on the mend now, thank goodness.'

'He's got huge dark rings round his eyes. Are you sleeping all right, Dennis?'

Dennis kept fidgeting with his hands while she was talking and wouldn't stand still, as if he was nervous about something.

'Answer the nice lady,' Mrs Gough rebuked, and he cleared his throat and whispered 'Yes, ma'am.'

'What do you do with your spare time, Dennis?'

'I try to be a help,' he said, his eyes to the floor, and Miss Edwards looked a bit surprised. 'I think you should take him to a doctor,' she told Mrs Gough. 'The council will pay. Just let me know how much it costs.'

'That's kind of you,' said Mrs Gough. 'It can be hard to manage with two growing boys to feed.'

The two women chatted for a while as Dennis and I stood to one side, then, when she finished her cup of tea, Miss Edwards looked at us again. 'So are you happy here, boys? Do you want to stay?' She smiled, encouragingly.

I could see Mrs Gough staring hard at us with a nasty glint in her eye and nodding her head, letting us know the answer she expected us to give.

'Yes, ma'am,' I said, and I think Dennis nodded. Inside I was miserable, though. I watched Miss Edwards pull on her coat and hat and walk out the front door and I wanted to run after her and shout 'No! Don't go! Don't leave us here!'

But I didn't. I didn't say anything. I was far too scared. No one could help us. We just had to get through it on our own somehow.

Chapter One

Once, when I was four years old, I climbed up onto the car deck of the big Transporter Bridge in Newport. It was fun up there because when all the cars had driven on, the deck started to move, carrying them over to the other side of the river. I had my feet dangling over the side, watching the boats down below, and I thought I was the bee's knees.

Suddenly a man in a uniform rushed up and grabbed me by the arm. He pulled me to my feet, hurting my shoulder, and shouted 'What do you think you're doing?'

'I was just looking,' I told him.

He said that I could have fallen and been killed and he wanted to know where my mam and dad lived, so I told him they lived on Bolt Street. My big brother Dennis had made me remember the address in case I ever got lost.

The man said that my mam and dad would be going crazy with worrying about me, but I didn't think they would. I usually went out for the whole day because Mam didn't like me to get under her feet. She was always fussing over my little brother Freddie, who was only two, and she let me do whatever I wanted.

The man with the uniform made me stand right beside him until the deck crossed back over the river again, then he told me to run straight home as fast as I could. 'Your mam will be making your tea soon,' he said to encourage me.

I was pretty hungry but I knew there wouldn't be any food back at the house. There hadn't been any that morning, at any rate. I wandered up through the dock area and picked up some stones to throw in the water, but another man came running over and told me off.

'What are you doing? You might fall in,' he shouted.

Everyone was telling me what to do all of a sudden.

He asked my name and I told him it was Terry.

'Fancy a biscuit, Terry?' he asked, and led me to a shed over in the corner of the dockyard where he gave me two whole Rich Tea biscuits, which weren't even broken. They tasted fantastic.

While I was eating them, he asked me if I came down that way often. He said he was usually there and I should look out for him so we could be friends. I thought to myself that he was far too old to be my friend but I didn't say anything because he had been nice to give me the biscuits.

I asked him the time and when he told me it was after three o'clock, I said I had to go. I always went up the road to meet Dennis coming out of school.

'Come back again another time,' the man said, and I thought to myself that I definitely would because it wasn't often someone gave you biscuits just like that.

I walked up to Bolt Street and sat on the pavement just down the road from the school, waiting for Dennis to come along. Loads of kids came out in a big crowd when the bell rang but I could always spot Dennis in the midst of them because he did a funny walk, with one foot in the gutter and one foot on the pavement, making him look as if he was limping. Every day he did that.

'What's up, Terry?' he asked when he got up close to me, and he ruffled up my hair.

'I went up on the Transporter Bridge and a man gave me two biscuits,' I told him straight away, then I felt guilty because really I should have kept one for Dennis. It's just that I was so hungry, I had eaten them both myself.

'What man?' Dennis asked.

'He's got a hut down at the docks.'

'I know who you mean.' Dennis frowned. 'He's a bit odd, that one. Best not go to his hut without me there, OK?'

'OK,' I shrugged. If Dennis said so, then I wouldn't.

'Want to go to the park now?' he asked, and I said yes and trotted off behind him, happy just to be in his company.

I missed Dennis now he was at school. Before that it had just been him and me going out on adventures together. We'd play hopscotch on the railway tracks, or walk along the top of the high stone wall down by the docks, or play hide and seek in the park, where they had a pavilion and a bandstand and rockeries and lots of good places to hide.

Dennis and I had always played together. My other brothers and sisters were too old, apart from Freddie, and he was too young. When I was four, Cyril was eighteen, Betty was sixteen, Charles was twelve, Tom was ten, Rose was eight and Dennis was six. The big ones thought I was a nuisance and were mean to me. They used to hang me upside down over the banisters to try and calm me down, but as soon as they set me on my feet again I'd yell at them that they were effing bastards and sprint off down the stairs before they could catch me. I liked saying 'effing' and 'bloody' and 'bastard', like my big brothers and my dad always did, but it used to make the girls cross with me.

In those days the coalman delivered coal to the houses by horse and cart and everyone would threaten that if I didn't behave myself, the coalman would take me away in his cart. He was a big, scary, soot-faced man with a loud voice so I'd cower in the background when he came to the door, just in case.

Some mams would cuddle their little boys – I'd seen them in our road – but our mam never did anything but shout at me, so I usually kept out of her way. Besides, she had a funny eye that gave me the creeps. She'd be looking at you with one eye but the other one would be off staring over your shoulder, which wasn't very nice to see.

I hardly ever saw my dad because he was never home. Mam said he was off working but Dennis whispered to me 'Yeah, if you count sitting in the pub lifting a pint of beer to your lips work, that is.'

Tom once told me that Dad had knocked a man out in a fight with just one punch and I was quite impressed about that. And there was a funny story about him when he was a kid. He'd sneaked downstairs in his family's pub in the middle of the night to try and pinch money from the jukebox, but he did something wrong and it suddenly blared out loud music, wakening everyone up. 'Oh, Oh, Antonio' the song was called. Dennis used to sing it for me and it made me laugh every time.

We moved home a lot when I was little. I think it was because Mam and Dad couldn't pay the rent. There were angry scenes on the doorstep with men demanding money and Mam telling them to eff off, then we would have to move again. I know I was born in Frederick Street, then at one point we lived in a wide road called Portland Street that had trees down the middle of it. Next we moved to a flat in Commercial Road, and the last place we were living in was Bolt Street. All these places were in Pillgwenlly, or 'Pill', as everyone called it, the area of Newport that led down to the docks. It wasn't posh round there. We didn't have much money but I don't think anyone else did either.

You don't miss what you've never had. I was starving a lot of the time, but I thought that's just what people had to put up with. I had itchy scabs all over my legs, but so did Dennis so it never occurred to me there was anything that could be done about them. It was freezing cold in winter, especially at night, when Dennis, Freddie and I huddled together under one blanket. But at least we had a roof over our heads and got fed mashed potatoes or watery stew or fried bread a couple of times a day.

My favourite times were when I was out playing with Dennis. He looked out for me and made sure I didn't get into trouble. I remember one day I caught my fingers in the door of the public toilets in the park and it hurt so much that I howled for ages. I sat on a wall outside crying my eyes out while Dennis tried to comfort me. It's funny the things that stick in your head. After he started school, I was really lonely during the day. I never wanted to hang around at home, with Mam shouting at me or arguing with Dad, so I just set off on my own in the morning and wandered round until it was time for Dennis to come out of school.

My brother Tom did his best to look out for us kids but he was too young to get a job so all he could do was busk at the coach station, scrounge food from the market, scrabble in bins for fruit and veg that had been thrown away, or simply beg. Sometimes he was so desperate that he would steal empty lemonade bottles so he could take them back to the shop for the deposit. When he had any money, he'd make sure we got a nice dinner, like stew and mash, and he would give Dad some cash for beer and cigarettes.

Tom should have been at school, though. He was always getting into trouble with the police for begging and other little things, but it was a huge shock to me when I heard he had been arrested and sent to remand school. The idea that the police could put you in handcuffs and lock you away made a big impression on me at the time. I found the whole idea terrifying. Would they be coming for me next? After that I used to hide whenever I saw a policeman coming towards me.

One morning in December 1939, just after my fifth birthday, a big tall man in a long coat came to our front door, carrying a briefcase and all kinds of papers. He said he was some kind of inspector and insisted that Mam should let him in. Something about his brusque manner worried me so I ran to hide behind the settee and peeped out timidly as he looked round our home.

'These floors are in a disgusting state,' he said to Mam. 'Don't you ever wash them?'

She was agitated. 'We're just about to move,' she told him. 'Things have been difficult because my husband's been out of work and we're behind with the rent, but he's signed up to the Army now and we've got a new place to go to and things will all be fine there.'

'But things aren't fine, Mrs O'Neill. Dennis and Rose have been sent home from school because of the sores on their legs. Have you done anything about that?'

'Yes, well, I'm going to take them to the clinic,' Mam said.

'And when were you planning to do that?'

Mam was really flustered now, covering her face with her hands so the Inspector had to tell her he couldn't hear what she was saying.

'Just as soon as I can,' she mumbled, then started crying. 'It's not easy with eight kids and no money coming in. You should try it.'

The Inspector had crouched down on the floor and was looking at Freddie. 'This boy has a terrible rash all over his chest,' he said, and I could see him drawing his hands back and putting them in his pocket as if he was scared of catching something. 'Where's your next youngest?' He consulted a piece of paper. 'Terence, isn't it?'

Mam looked around and caught sight of me cowering behind the settee. 'There he is.' She pointed.

Next thing, the Inspector leaned over and grabbed me by the arm and hauled me out, kicking and cursing.

'Get off me, you! Leave me alone.'

He held me just long enough to get a look at my snotty nose – I always seemed to have a cold in those days – and the itchy scabs all over my legs.

'I'm going to get a doctor to come and look at these children,' he said. 'They need medical treatment.'

He stood up and wrote something on his papers and then made for the door. 'I'll return later, Mrs O'Neill,' he said. 'Make sure all the children are here when I get back.'

After he left, Mam sat sobbing on the settee. I wanted to run out the door and escape but Dennis talked me out of it.

'Maybe the doctor will give us something to stop the itching,' he said. 'That'd be good, wouldn't it?'

I wasn't convinced, but if Dennis was staying, I decided I would as well.

When the doctor came later with his big black medical bag, I noticed he wore gloves to examine us, as if we were too dirty to touch. We lined up in front of him and one by one he listened to our chests and looked at our arms and legs and peered into our ears and eyes. The Inspector stood behind him with his arms folded.

After a while the doctor stood up. 'The four youngest children need hospital treatment,' he said. 'They'll never get better in these conditions.' He looked around the room. 'I'll arrange for them to be picked up.'

'Where are you taking them?' Mam cried. 'I don't know what their father will have to say about this.'

'Just to St Woolos hospital, Mrs O'Neill. We'll sort them out there and they'll be home before you know it.' He glanced at the Inspector. 'We'll be in touch to let you know, at any rate.'

I looked at Dennis and he didn't seem to be bothered by this turn of events. 'We'll get lots of grub in hospital,' he whispered to me. 'And I won't have to go to school.'

But the doctor and the Inspector were big scary men and I was worried that they were going to put me in handcuffs and lock me away, as they had done to Tom, so when they came to pick us up I tried to hide and I was screaming my head off as they dragged me out into a van parked in the street outside. Freddie was crying too, but Rose and Dennis were sitting quietly so I soon calmed down, following their lead.

When we got to the hospital, the first thing I saw was a big grand front doorway with wide steps, which to me seemed really posh. We were taken up to the ward in a lift with criss-cross metal gates that clanked shut. I giggled when I first saw the nurses because they looked so funny with big white caps that were like boats perched on top of their heads. They gave us all hot baths, then one of them painted brown liquid all over my skin, from neck to toes, and I wriggled when she got to the ticklish bits. They were nice, those nurses: smiling and gentle and good fun.

The four of us were put in the same ward, each with our own bed, which was a luxury I'd never experienced before. I loved the feel of the crisp white sheets and the clean, starchy smell and the fact that I had my own little bedside cupboard, despite having nothing to put in it. At mealtimes, a trolley came round with fantastic food, the likes of which I'd never tried before. There were chunks of real meat in the stews, and mashed turnips and puddings with creamy yellow custard. One day we had tripe cooked in milk and Rose wouldn't eat it because she said it was disgusting, that it was made from cows' stomachs, but I thought it was very tasty.

It was Christmas while we were in hospital and we got a special dinner that day with turkey and stuffing and roast potatoes, which was the best meal I'd ever had in my life. Everyone was in a good mood. The nurses tied lots of balloons round Freddie's bed and tried to teach him how to sing 'Run, rabbit, run, rabbit, run, run, run'. We all laughed till our sides hurt as he tried to copy them because at not-quite-three years old he couldn't pronounce the letter 'R' so it came out as 'Wun, wabbit'. It was a really happy day.

We stayed in St Woolos hospital for a few weeks, and the rash on my skin cleared up rapidly. It was great not to be scratching my legs till they bled the whole time. The matron also gave me medicines to help clear my chest, and my nose stopped running constantly, which was a welcome relief. Then one day we were told to get dressed in the clothes we'd arrived in, which had been washed and pressed for us. Dennis, Rose and I lined up at the end of our beds, and watched as the Inspector came into the ward and greeted the nurses.

'Are we all ready?' he said to us.

We nodded.

'Good,' he said. 'Off we go.'

I was sad leaving the ward because I'd really liked the nurses and the lovely food and having my own bed. I assumed we were being taken back home again to sleeping crushed up in a rough old bed and feeling hungry most of the time.

'What about Freddie?' Dennis asked, and was told he would be following on later.

Dennis and I were ushered into a van outside, but Rose went off separately. No one told us where she was going. No one told us where we were going either, but instead of taking us back towards Pillgwenlly, I realized we were being driven into the centre of Newport and soon we pulled up outside a great big house on the top of Stow Hill.

'What are we doing here?' Dennis asked.

'This is your new home,' the Inspector told us. 'For a while at any rate. It's a children's home. You'll be looked after here until we decide what we're going to do with you next. Be good boys, mind, and I'm sure you'll like it.'

I looked up at the big, smart-looking building set in nice gardens and I decided that if it was anything like the hospital, that would be OK with me. I didn't mind if we weren't going home. I didn't miss Mam or my older brothers or sister. The only person I cared about – Dennis – was there with me and with him around, everything was sure to be fine.

Chapter Two

I didn't realize there was a war on until I got to Stow Hill Children's Home in January 1940, despite the fact that my dad had signed up to fight. Somehow it hadn't got through to me that Hitler had invaded Poland and we had declared war on Germany as a result. I was only five years old, so that's my excuse. But one of the first things we learned at Stow Hill was that when the air-raid warning sounded it meant there were German planes in the sky and we had to run to the shelter in case they dropped a bomb on us.

If the sirens sounded during the day, we ran to the shelter entrance which was in the big yard surrounded by a high wall where we played at the back of the building. If they went off at night, we had to leave our bedroom and file down the stairs to the front room where there was a trap door in the floor, just in front of the fireplace. When you opened the trap door, stairs led down to the cellar below. There were bunk beds down there where we waited until the all-clear sounded. I never minded being in there because it was cosy and warm and we were all perfectly comfortable. It was scary to think that enemy aeroplanes could be dropping bombs up above and I shivered at the thought of being caught upstairs when it happened.

'Denny, what if I'm in the lav when the siren goes off and I don't hear it?' I asked.

'I'd come and get you, stupid,' he said, cuffing the back of my head.

One of the boys in the home had an uncanny knack of imitating the sound of the air-raid siren. It was so realistic that it was practically impossible to tell the difference from the real thing. One night when everyone was asleep and all was quiet, he decided to have a bit of fun and let rip with his air-raid sound. Seconds later the supervisors were racing around herding us all down the stairs and through the trap door to the shelter. They must have wondered why we were all sniggering to ourselves as word got around about who had sounded the alarm, but I don't think they ever found out they'd been tricked.

Stow Hill wasn't a huge children's home; it was more of a reception centre where they put children while they decided what to do with them. There were probably only five or six boys staying there apart from us. The house had three or four big bedrooms, and Dennis and I were in adjoining beds; when Freddie arrived from hospital he came in beside us. One of the bedrooms was occupied by two old ladies, who were always roasting chestnuts in front of the fire. I remember the sweet, nutty smell which pervaded the house, but they never offered us boys any of them. I don't think I ever talked to them. They kept themselves to themselves.

Rationing was brought in the month we arrived at Stow Hill, and meat was one of the first things to be restricted, but I don't remember us going short. We had bread (but no jam), porridge (but no sugar to put on it), potatoes, fish, vegetables (but little fresh fruit). My sisters Rose and Betty turned up at the home one day bringing us some apples and oranges, and I found out later that Betty had nicked them from a greengrocer's. After that, Dennis and I always referred to it as 'the forbidden fruit'. It wasn't an official visit. They sneaked in through a back door to the home that opened onto an alley and crept around until they found us playing in the yard.

'Where are you staying now?' I asked Rose as I took a big bite of my apple, juice trickling down my chin.

'At Grandmother's,' she said.

My mam's mam lived in another part of Newport. I wondered why Rose got to stay with her but we didn't.

'She's only got room for me,' Rose explained.

Betty told us that she was staying at home with Mam but she was joining the Women's Land Army and working on a farm. I thought that sounded like fun.

'You're lucky because you don't have to go to school,' Rose said.

It was true. Our days in Stow Hill were spent playing in the yard out the back, but there was a limit to the number of games we could get up to without any toys. I missed the freedom of the days when I went wandering down to the docks or crossed the river on the Transporter Bridge, but we had been told firmly that we weren't allowed out of the home and I for one obeyed the rules, because I had discovered to my horror what would happen if I didn't.

One night, a couple of weeks after we arrived, I was in the bath when the young woman who was supervising my bath-time suddenly picked up a big wooden bath brush and hit me across the back with it.

I screamed in shock and tried to jump out of the bath and run away but she gripped my arm so tightly I couldn't escape.

'Don't you go cheeking me, young Terence,' she said, and brought the bath brush down again on my skinny frame.

I burst into hysterical crying, struggling to release my arm. I had no idea what I had said to upset her – I hadn't thought I was being cheeky. No one had ever hit me in my life before. Mam and Dad might have neglected us but at least they didn't beat us. I'm still not exactly sure what she was cross about.

'Stop your whining,' she snapped and hit me for a third time, across the shoulders, and I howled in pain.

When she let go of me, I curled up in a ball at the end of the bath, crying so hard I had a coughing fit and nearly choked.

'For goodness sake, be a big boy!' she snapped. 'It wasn't that bad.'

But to me it was. The shock of a painful blow coming out of the blue like that was horrible. When I told Dennis later, he said that he had been hit as well and that we would just have to try to stay out of trouble. But how could I when I didn't know what I had done wrong in the first place?

After that, I was hit several more times at Stow Hill and I usually didn't have a clue what I'd done to deserve it. Punishments were dished out for the slightest reason and you never knew when the next one was coming your way. I tried to be good and follow the rules, but still I got hit. The injustice of it bothered me a lot but there was no one I could complain to except Dennis, and there was nothing he could do about it.

One day a boy in our room had an ingenious idea. He attached a small plastic bucket to the end of a broom handle using a length of string, then he lowered the bucket over the high wall at the back of the house, so it was dangling above the pavement below. As people walked past on the street, they dropped pennies into his bucket until it was heavy with coins. Unfortunately, just as he pulled it back over into the yard, one of the officials in the home saw him and, because Dennis and I had been standing watching, we got punished as well – which seemed most unfair to me.

'But we weren't doing anything,' I cried, unable to contain my rage. If I had done something naughty, fair enough, but I hadn't.

'Be quiet! Don't talk back!' the supervisor snapped and hit me again.

A hard little core of defiance formed inside me. I hated unfairness. I thought these people were nasty and tried to stay out of their way, keeping my head down so I didn't draw attention to myself. How dare they hit Dennis and me! How dare they!

The months went by, and in May 1940 an official told us that there had been a court case to talk about our future, and that they had decided we would be best looked after by the local authority rather than going back home to Mam again. She and Betty were on their own at the time because Dad was over fighting in France against the Nazis. During that May, Dennis told me that Dad had been one of the thousands of soldiers evacuated from Dunkirk as the German army approached. Seemingly he had to spend a long time up to his neck in oily waters off the French coast and he claimed his health never recovered after that.

I didn't care about the fact that we weren't going home. I'd never had any feelings for my mam. I didn't even call her 'mam' – I never talked to her – so I certainly didn't miss her. I was happy enough at Stow Hill, apart from when someone hit me. However, our time there wasn't going to last forever. We were told by one of the staff in the home that the welfare officers had put an advert in the paper seeking foster parents for 'three Catholic boys', and they had received eleven replies. They spent some time interviewing all the prospective candidates, then in October 1940 it was decided that we would be sent to stay with a couple called Mr and Mrs Sorrel, who lived a few miles outside Hereford, which I found out was over the border in England.

Dennis, Freddie and I were looking forward to going to our new home. We reckoned that they must be kind people to take us on and that they'd probably give us lots of presents and lovely meals. We fantasized about how nice their house would be, and how it would be like having a real mam and dad to look after us, instead of the useless ones we had had before.

However, when the day came to travel to the Sorrels, I had a high temperature and wasn't allowed to go. Dennis and Freddie set off without me, and I was most upset and indignant about it. I had to spend a week at Stow Hill all on my own, lying in bed and swallowing horrible medicines. The following Saturday they came back to collect me along with Mrs Sorrel, an old lady with grey hair and a friendly face.

We got on a bus to take us the fifty-mile journey from Newport to Hereford and, as we boarded, I did something very naughty. Maybe I was bored after my week's confinement to bed. Maybe I was jealous that Dennis and

Freddie had gone ahead of me. Or maybe I just fancied the piles of bus tickets sitting under a clipboard, all of them in different colours to denote their different values. While the conductor wasn't looking, I lifted the spring, slipped one of the piles out of its place and shoved it into my coat pocket.

It wasn't long before the conductor noticed one of his piles of tickets was missing and there was a great hulla-baloo. He made the driver stop the bus and everyone was asked to look on the floor at their feet to see if they could find the lost tickets. I pretended to look along with every-one else, chuckling to myself about the loot in my pocket. Of course, the tickets weren't found and the bus contin-ued on its way.

When we got to the Sorrels' house, a pretty old cottage in its own grounds on the edge of a small village, I took off my coat and threw it on a chair. The movement must have jiggled the pack of bus tickets because Dennis suddenly spotted them poking out.

'Here, Terry! What's this all about then?' he asked, pulling them out.

I thought he would think it was a good laugh and would share in the joke with me, but instead, to my horror, he shouted for Mrs Sorrel.

'Look at this! Our Terry's been thieving,' he shouted. 'He's got the bus tickets.'

She came out of the kitchen and looked at me sadly. 'Oh, Terence, how could you? We'll have to take these back to the bus station tomorrow and apologize. What were you thinking?'

I braced myself for a punishment of some kind but it didn't happen. She just seemed really disappointed in me and that made me ashamed. I hadn't thought I was doing any harm, but Mrs Sorrel said that stealing is stealing no matter whether it's a gold sovereign or a halfpenny piece. I was upset that she had a bad opinion of me from the very first day I arrived there. It wasn't a good start.

I was furious with Dennis for ratting on me as well, and later on we had a scrap in the garden when I called him a dirty rat and a bloody tell-tale and a traitor. We quite often scrapped, in the way that brothers do, wrestling each other to the ground and giving dead arms and legs, but we never really hurt each other. Dennis was much stronger than me and he'd pin me down on the ground so I couldn't fight any more and that's usually how it ended.

The Sorrels had a great garden for kids to play in. An overgrown path led down to an old brick toilet and then there was a brass bedstead sticking out of the boundary hedge, which Mr Sorrel said helped to keep the foxes out. And best of all, just across a field there was an old aerodrome and we could watch the planes taking off and landing, which was very exciting for three young boys. One of the pilots from the base sometimes came over to the Sorrels' for his tea and Dennis and I used to ply him with questions about how many bombs he had dropped and what it was like being chased through the skies by enemy planes.

Dennis and I slept in an attic room in the cottage, and we had to climb a ladder to go to bed at night, which was an adventure for lads our age. On bath nights, Mrs Sorrel put an old tin bath in front of the open fire and then heated a big cauldron over the flames to get hot water. Freddie would have his bath first, then me, and then Dennis, but between each of us she topped up the bath with hot water from the cauldron. No one had ever been so kind to me in my life up to that date. I'd lie back in the steaming water thinking 'This is the life!'

During the week, Dennis went to a village school that was just across the road from the cottage but I didn't start there, despite the fact I was almost six. I don't know why. During the day, I just played out in the garden with Freddie and sometimes we helped Mr Sorrel to tend his vegetables. There was a lake nearby with swans on it so we might go to look at them. On Sundays we all attended the local church, which was the first time I'd been to church in my life. I found it a bit boring and was always being reprimanded for fidgeting during the sermon. The priest used big words and I could never understand what he was talking about so it was hard to sit still.

I was pretty happy there with the Sorrels. They were nice people, salt of the earth you might say, but I think they found three energetic boys a bit of a handful. I was already getting a reputation for being the naughty one of the three, although I don't think I was naughty so much as restless when I got bored. I do remember that I was always being told off for using colourful language, which I had picked up from my dad and my older brothers back at home. Everyone swore in Bolt Street; that's just the way they talked.

Anyway, come the New Year of 1941, a welfare officer arrived and told us we were moving on again and that we would be picked up on the 6th to go to our next home. It seemed we had only just arrived and started to get settled, and that was my main objection to the move. Although the Sorrels had been nice, I hadn't had time in the three months to become attached to either of them. I just thought it would have been better if we could have put down roots somewhere instead of being always in temporary places. But it wasn't up to me. That much was clear already. I just had to do as I was told and go wherever the council took me.

Chapter Three

A man from Newport Council came to pick us up and take us to our next home, in the village of Yarpole near Leominster. After we got off the bus, we had to follow him on foot along some very narrow lanes, where frost sparkled on the tarmac and our breath misted the air. The last part of the walk was uphill and Freddie, who was still only three, kept falling behind so we had to shout at him to hurry up.

At last we reached a big black and white house surrounded by railings and set back in huge gardens. The council man opened a tall metal gate and led us up a long crazy-paving path to a huge wooden front door. He lifted the door knocker and knocked with a loud clattering sound and shortly afterwards a maid in a black dress with a white apron opened the door.

'Come in,' she said. 'I'll tell the lady of the house that you've arrived.'

Dennis and I stared at each other, mouths wide open. The hall was oak-panelled with paintings hung on the walls and the highest ceilings I'd ever seen. An oak staircase lined with more pictures curled up to the next floor.

The maid reappeared and ushered us through a door into a living room that was bigger than our entire flat in Bolt Street. A posh lady with lots of wavy silver hair and smart clothes was standing by the fireplace looking at us.

'This is Mrs Connop,' the council man told us; then he introduced us to her one by one. We didn't say anything, still too much in awe of the grand surroundings. To us, it was like somewhere a king and queen might live. All it lacked was a throne.

'Go and wait outside in the hall, boys, while Mrs Connop and I have a talk,' he told us.

We turned and trouped back out to the hall obediently.

'Are we really going to stay here?' I whispered to Dennis. 'It's like a castle or something.'

'Looks that way,' he replied.

'This is far better than the Sorrels. We've landed on our feet this time,' I said, gazing round.

Dennis shrugged. 'If things don't change, they'll stay as they are,' he said mysteriously, and I thought it sounded like an impossibly clever thing to say.

We could hear voices inside the sitting room but couldn't make out what they were saying. I wasn't tempted to put my ear against the door though. I'd already got used to the fact that grown-ups we barely knew made all the decisions about where we stayed and who looked after us. It wasn't up to us. We just had to go with the flow and do what they told us to.

After a while, the council man popped his head out. 'Come on in, boys,' he said, smiling. 'I'm delighted to say that Mrs Connop has agreed that you can come and live here. This is your new home. Say thank you to her.'

'Thank you,' we all mumbled.

'Now you have to promise that you will behave yourselves, and look out for each other,' he said. 'Do you promise?'

We said that we did, and shortly afterwards he hurried off to catch the bus back all the way to Newport, his job done.

Mrs Connop told us to sit down, so we huddled together on her big comfortable sofa, three sets of skinny thighs poking out of grey shorts all lined up on her lovely soft cushions. She told us that her husband, Mr Connop, and her youngest son James were outside working on the farm that adjoined the house and that they'd be back for dinner later. She explained that her two eldest sons, Michael and John, were in the Air Force, and that her daughter, Olga, was in the Forces as well. We were to address her and her husband as 'Ma'am' and 'Sir', and the boys as 'Master', but I can't remember what we were supposed to call Olga. Maybe she didn't mention that.

She said there was a lodger, a distant relative of hers, who lived in a room off the main hall, and she told us that the maid who'd ushered us in earlier would be the person who looked after us.

Then there was a list of rules we had to remember: we were only to use the back stairs, not the grand ones we'd seen outside in the hall; we would eat our meals in the kitchen, not the main dining room, which was just for family members; and she said that Dennis and I would be starting school just as soon as she could get us enrolled. That all sounded fair enough. She said it in a kind way, smiling at us, and when she'd finished she picked up a little bell on the table beside her and rang it to summon the maid to come and show us to our rooms.

The maid was a girl in her early twenties with a mass of bright red hair, so it wasn't long before Dennis and I started calling her Ginger, which she didn't seem to mind. She was a laughing, friendly type who was always generous to us, making sure we had plenty to eat and telling us gossip about the local area. She was more like a friend than someone in charge of us, and we all adored her from the word go.

We ate our meals with Ginger, sitting at the big kitchen table, and when she heard the bell ring she would dash through to the dining room to collect the dishes that the family had been eating from. That first evening there was rice pudding, one of my favourite foods of all time. When Ginger brought through the family's empty pudding dishes, I noticed that they had left the skin on the sides of their plates, which to me was crazy because I thought that was the best bit.

'Can I scrape the plates?' I begged Ginger.

'No, can I?' pleaded Dennis, his eyes spotting what mine had already noticed.

When she realized what we wanted, Ginger solved the dispute by scraping the plates herself and dividing the delicious baked skin between the three of us.

After dinner, we were taken in to the sitting room to meet Mr Connop. We stood in a row with our heads bowed, hands behind our backs, not sure what to expect.

'Come over here, Freddie,' he said. 'Do you want a sweet?' He held out his two closed fists. 'Which hand do you think the sweet is in?'

Freddie pointed to one of his hands and he opened it to show a boiled sweet in its cellophane wrapper. Freddie swiftly unwrapped the sweet and popped it in his mouth, so his little cheek bulged out to the side.

'You next! Terence, is it?'

I picked one of his fists and took the sweet inside it, then Dennis did the same. But what a shock I got when I opened the cellophane wrapper and popped the sweet in my mouth!

'Pah!' I spat it out into my hand. 'Yuck!' Instead of the sugary taste I'd been waiting for, my mouth was filled with the taste of soap.

Mr Connop roared with laughter. 'You got the trick one, Terence. Weren't expecting that, were you?'

I stood, crestfallen, until he pulled another sweet, a real one, out of his pocket and handed it to me.

'Be on your guard in future,' he said. 'You never know when someone might be having a joke with you.' He winked, knowingly.

The next day Mr Connop played another joke on us. He led us into the dining room, where his radio set was playing some music, and told us to sit down and not move a muscle. We all sat as we'd been instructed and he left the room, closing the door behind him. We waited and waited and then there was a loud knock on the door. The three of us looked at each other.

'Should we answer it?' I asked.

Dennis shrugged and we waited, but then the knocking came again. I decided it might be someone needing a hand with something, so I got up and opened the door to find Mr Connop standing outside.

'Hah!' he pointed. 'You'd never make it in the army if you can't obey a simple order! I said to sit still and not move a muscle.' Then he burst out laughing at his own trick.

He was always the joker in the house. In the morning we'd quite often hear him walking along the corridor outside our room, letting out what we thought were loud farts with every step. How could anyone fart that much? I was amazed that such a posh person could be so rude. It was only when I peeked out the door one day I realized he wasn't breaking wind at all. They were armpit farts, which are caused by placing the palm of your hand over your armpit and moving it up and down to create suction. He giggled like a schoolboy when I caught him out. I thought it was such a good trick that I practised and practised myself until I had mastered the art of armpit farts.

Mrs Connop was much stricter, telling us off for making too much noise as we ran down the hall, or tramping mud into the house, or splashing water in the bathroom, but she was always fair. When she told me off I always knew she had good reason to, and that was far better than the system at Stow Hill where punishments had been arbitrary and unexpected.

About a week after we arrived at the Connops, it was time for Dennis and me to start school, and because Newport Education Authority had said that we were to be brought up as Roman Catholics, we were enrolled at the Sisters of Charity School at nearby Croft Castle. Well, I say 'nearby' but in fact it was about four miles away from the Connops' house. Every morning we had to set out through the village to the lodge gates and then up a long school driveway lined with huge beech trees that creaked and swayed in the wind. I didn't mind the morning walk so much, although it meant getting up at the crack of dawn so we'd be there on time. What I hated was the walk home after dark in those winter days, listening to the wind whistling through the branches. The moon shining through the bare trees cast strange shadows on the ground and we could hear the sounds of dogs howling and owls hooting, which made our imaginations work overtime.

'There's a bogeyman lives in these woods,' Dennis told me. 'He eats young boys for breakfast and spits out their bones.'

I was quite a cocky six-year-old and didn't scare easily, but these walks would frighten the life out of me. I'd run as fast as I could to get past the eery stretch of trees, through the lodge gates and out into the open, and Dennis would come running after me laughing but, if truth be told, more than a little scared himself. The following year, after Freddie started school, I'd do the same thing to him, telling him stories about the blood-thirsty bogeyman until he was almost hysterical with fear.

In spring and summer it was a different matter and we really enjoyed our walks to school. It was beautiful countryside, carpeted with bluebells in spring, and we passed by a small lake where watercress grew round the edges in summer. Dennis and I often picked bunches of watercress and took them home, where Ginger would make us delicious watercress sandwiches for tea. It tasted lovely in white crusty bread fresh from the oven. Mrs Connop made her own bread every week, using a long pole with a flat bit on the end to push the tins of dough into fiery bread ovens, then pulling them out again when the bread was baked. We loved watching her doing it, partly because the smell was so fantastic.

There was one downside of summer on that farm, though, which I discovered to my horror at tea one night. Up above the kitchen table, haunches of pig were covered in salt and suspended on wooden racks to cure and become bacon. I was sitting right beneath one with a bowl of vegetable soup that Ginger had just handed me. Suddenly there was a plopping sound as something fell into my soup. At first I thought Dennis had thrown something at me and I looked up suspiciously but he was busy with his own soup. What could it be? There was another 'plop' and when I looked into my bowl I could see a little white worm-like thing wriggling away.

'Agh!' I shrieked. 'Ginger, what's that?'

She peered over. 'That's a maggot,' she told me, matter-of-factly. 'Flies lay their eggs up there in the bacon on any bits that aren't covered by salt, and maggots are the result. Good source of protein if you fancy eating them!' She laughed at the horror on my face. 'Either that or just keep your bowl covered up next time.'

All three of us quickly put our arms round our soup bowls and leaned over to protect them, and for the rest of the summer we would always check our food carefully before taking a bite.

At weekends and during school holidays we went out to help Mr Connop and James on the farm, although I'm not sure how much help we were at our age. There weren't any tractors in those days so horses had to pull the ploughs and it was one of our jobs to take the horses to the drinking troughs for water and help to feed them. One Saturday I worked in a field with Mr Connop for the whole day, hoeing the crops row by row, and at teatime he slapped me on the back and told me I was a really good worker. I liked his praise and decided I was going to try and earn it whenever I could. I looked up to him and wished he could be my real dad and not just my foster dad because I wanted to be like him when I grew up.

The next day, he asked the three of us to collect the thistles that had been cut in one of the orchards. I decided to try and build a 'thistle-rick', copying the way I'd seen the grown-ups building hayricks. I filled a wheelbarrow full of thistles and started pushing it along the rutted ground, but it was way too big and heavy for me.

Mrs Connop saw what I was trying to do and, trying to spare me, she called out that I should put the wheelbarrow away and come indoors to get ready for school the next morning.

I hated to fail at anything I set out to do, and I was yearning for Mr Connop to praise me again, so I was feeling a bit upset and frustrated as I turned to take the wheelbarrow back to the shed. The wheel hit a stone and got stuck and, instead of trying to move round it, in a fit of temper I shoved the wheelbarrow up against the stone trying to force it over. At that moment, my foot slipped and I lost my balance and fell, hitting my face hard on the edge of the metal wheelbarrow.

Mrs Connop came flying across the field to pick me up. My mouth was full of hot, salty liquid and when I spat it out, I was alarmed to see bright red blood all over the ground and down the front of my shirt.

'Your teeth!' Mrs Connop wailed. I looked down and, sure enough, there were my two front teeth on the ground. I felt with my tongue and there was just a big ragged gap where they used to be. Thankfully it was only my baby teeth I lost, but I had a year or so of being teased by all and sundry about the gap. I became so self-conscious about it that I used to cover my mouth with my hand when I smiled or laughed. 'The toothless wonder,' Dennis used to call me. Needless to say, I wasn't allowed to use that wheelbarrow again.

The Sisters of Charity School was a boarding school as well as a day school and, as the name suggests, it was extremely religious. It had been a girls'-only school but by the time we got there, there were quite a few boys as well. I had to go to mass every morning, taking the communion wafer. We were taught by nuns, who used their best endeavours to turn us into holy creatures of the Lord and sometimes this involved rapping us on the knuckles with a ruler if we committed a sin such as using bad language or taking His name in vain. I was still a frequent, though inadvertent offender. Swear words just slipped out my mouth without me consciously putting them there.

Although Dad's family were Catholic, we'd never been to church back in Newport. My only religious experience was of the boring sermons at the Sorrels' church, but I was impressed by the elaborate ceremony of the Catholic church in Yarpole and thought there must be something in it all. I learned my lessons faithfully and after a few months I was dressed up in a white suit and had my confirmation by the priest, about which I was very proud.

On the way to and from school I had a bit of bother with some of the village kids bullying me. I don't know if it was my gappy teeth, or the fact that I was a welfare boy, or maybe just because I could be a bit mouthy, but I'd often find a group of them surrounding me and calling me names or chasing me down the road, throwing stones.

'Get off him,' Dennis would shout, charging towards us and hitting out at my attackers. 'Leave him alone, you little bastards.' Given that he was a good six inches taller than them, they'd usually melt away at that point. 'You OK?' he'd ask me gruffly, and I'd grin: 'Course I am!'

Dennis never hesitated to step in and protect me, despite the fact that he was the quieter, shyer one of the two of us. I was the tough one, ready to take on any challengers – and I frequently did.

I was glad when school broke up for the summer. The farm was a paradise for young boys and we spent hours on end out in the fields playing. We'd lie down in great mounds of freshly cut grass to make an imprint of our bodies, or we'd climb trees and collect eggs from birds' nests (although we knew never to take more than one egg from each nest so the mother didn't abandon it altogether). We'd make a hole at each end of an egg using a thorn from a thorn bush and blow out the white and the yolk to stop it going bad, then take it back to our bedroom. We didn't have many eggs but we were very proud of our little collection.

Perhaps our favourite game was aeroplanes and gliders. Dennis would tie one end of a long piece of string round his waist then attach the other round mine with a slip knot. He was the plane and I was the glider being towed around by him. We spent many happy hours running around the fields with our arms outstretched, Dennis going one way and me gliding the other, until we fell over exhausted on a grassy bank to lie and watch planes going overhead. Every young boy in those days knew the different markings you got on aeroplanes, and we were always on the lookout for ones with the tell-tale black-edged cross symbol that would indicate a stray German bomber. We never saw one, though, out there in the heart of Herefordshire. The war hardly impinged on our lives at all, since we didn't suffer any food shortages, being lucky enough to live on a farm. The most dangerous thing that happened to us that summer of 1941 was the day when Freddie nearly drowned.

It was a scorching hot day and the three of us had gone to play near the pond in one of the bottom fields, next to the orchard. There were tadpoles and frog-spawn in the water and we liked to collect it in glass jam jars. At the edge of the pond there was a big log, and Freddie decided to clamber out on it so he could get closer to the tadpoles, but just as he reached the furthest point, the log rolled over and tipped him into the deep water.

Immediately Dennis and I scrambled onto the log and lay full length along it, trying to catch his hand to pull him up again but it was difficult because he was struggling so much. He kept disappearing under the glassy green surface and we'd haul him back up coughing and spluttering. Neither of us could go in the water to help him because we couldn't swim. No one had ever taught us. We clutched at Freddie's hand, his clothes, panicking like mad as his fingers slithered yet again out of our grasp. 'Hold him!' I yelled at Dennis. 'I'm trying!' he yelled back. Finally we managed to get a firm grip and drag him back to shore, pulling him up through the weeds and mud.

There was a terrifying moment when he lay on the bank with his eyes closed, not moving. I shook him frantically, yelling 'Freddie! Wake up!' Dennis pushed down on his chest and pumped his hands up and down. And then Freddie coughed, and gasped for air, and when he started sobbing I knew he would be all right and I was flooded with relief.

'Thank God! Thank God!' I cried, shivering despite the heat. But then there was another worry. 'Mrs Connop will kill us when she finds out.'

'We can dry out his clothes before we go back,' Dennis decided. 'She doesn't need to know.'

We persuaded Freddie to take all his clothes off and laid them out on the banks to dry. He stopped crying and started chortling with glee at being able to run around the field stark naked.

We stayed out at the pond all day so that by the time we went back to the house, Freddie's clothes were dry, albeit caked in mud. We'd agreed we wouldn't tell Mrs Connop what had happened but Dennis was a bit of a tell-tale and couldn't seem to help himself. As soon as we saw her he blurted out 'Freddie fell in the pond.' She didn't get cross, though, because it was obvious that no harm had been done. I don't think she ever realized how close that four-year-old boy in her care had come to drowning.

It gave me a horrible fright, though. When I lay in bed later that night, I had visions of his little face disappearing under the murky water, only his hands still waving in the air. At breakfast the next morning, I looked at his blond hair and baby features and shuddered to think that he could have been dead. Freddie seemed to have forgotten all about it but those moments when he lay unconscious on the bank were lodged in my memory forever. They introduced a touch of something dark and menacing into the otherwise perfect boys'-own summer on the farm.

Chapter Four

It's fair to say I was no angel as a young lad. I think I had a natural curiosity about the world that got me into trouble. I also had sticky fingers when it came to things I was interested in, and that's another quality that tended to get me into scrapes.

There was a music room in a Portakabin behind the school where they kept lots of instruments for the school band: drums, cymbals, triangles and so forth. Although I wasn't particularly musical, I took a fancy to these instruments and started taking them home with me, one by one. A drum was first. Once I'd successfully sneaked it out of the school, I was quite brazen about it, banging it loudly all the way back to the Connops'.

'The nuns said I could have it,' I lied to Mrs Connop, and she took my word for it and didn't question me any further.

Next I took the triangle, and again said that the nuns had given me permission. It wasn't until I had virtually the whole instrument collection in my bedroom that Mrs Connop thought to contact the school, who told her that I hadn't been given permission to take them at all and that, in fact, they'd been on the point of calling in the police to investigate their disappearance. I had to return them and I got a double punishment because the nuns gave me a rap on the knuckles with a ruler for being a thief, and Mrs Connop gave me a whacking with a stick broken from an apple tree for lying to her.

It wasn't the only time I was caught pilfering at school. The teachers used to keep a supply of sweets in a cupboard to reward children who had been especially good during the day. I would sneak in at dinnertime and help myself to them, and I got away with it for quite some time before I was caught. It seemed to me that crime paid because all those sweets I'd had were well worth the single rap on the knuckles I received.

Mrs Connop's punishments were a bit more uncomfortable. I had to bend over and take six of the best on my backside, briskly delivered with a bendy stick, and I wasn't keen on that at all. I'd try to run away but she'd always catch up with me in the end. You couldn't win. Once, she bent me over one of the sacks of flour in the scullery where her bread ovens were kept and started whacking me. I saw a mouse inside the sack and reached in to grab it, thinking I'd use it to scare her. All women

40

were scared of mice, weren't they? I got my comeuppance, though, because the mouse bit me on the finger and I still got the whacking as well.

I don't think I ever got away with anything at the house. When Mrs Connop found that someone had been up to mischief, she'd call us into the room and demand to know who it was. Although all three of us would protest our innocence, I had an annoying habit of blushing so she would assume it was me, whether it was or not. Either that or Dennis would tell tales on me. I don't know why he did it. Maybe he thought she would like him better if he kept in her good books by sucking up to her.

Every morning, Mr Connop would knock to waken us for school and we were supposed to get up and wash then dress ourselves before going down for breakfast. One morning it was bitterly cold and I decided to get dressed sitting in bed, with my feet still under the covers to keep them warm. To me it was a clever plan and I couldn't see any harm in it. However, when we got downstairs, Dennis decided to tell Mrs Connop – 'Terry got dressed in his bed, under the covers' – and she went berserk. She grabbed me by the scruff of the neck and started dragging me into the scullery, where she kept a stick ready for beating me.

'You little so-and-so,' she yelled. 'Why is it always you who has to break the rules? Why can't you be a good boy like your brothers?'

At that point I struggled and managed to break free. I ran out the back door and down the path, with Mrs Connop in hot pursuit.

'Come back right now!' she yelled.

'No, I won't, 'cos you're going to hit me,' I shouted back.

'I promise I won't hit you,' she said, so I stopped and walked back towards her, but as soon as I was within reach she grabbed me by the collar and frogmarched me up to the house, giving me an earbashing about how there was a right way to do things and a wrong way. I still couldn't understand why it was such a huge crime to get dressed in bed on a cold morning, but she was a very strict, formal type of a person who liked everything done properly.

Sometimes I knew I was definitely in the wrong and on those occasions I'd take my punishment without complaint. Once I found a shotgun out in the barn, and for a laugh I picked it up and pointed it at Dennis and Freddie, threatening to shoot them. Just at that moment, a big black crow flew past and I turned to aim at it instead, which was just as well because the shotgun suddenly went off with a huge explosion that knocked me backwards onto the ground. People came running from all directions and I got royally whacked for that stunt. I hardly felt my punishment, though. I was still in too much shock about the fact that I could have killed one of my brothers if it had gone off a few seconds earlier. My ears were ringing from the blast for the rest of the day.

We didn't hear much about the bombing raids that were flattening British cities that year, but we were regularly warned that if we saw something that looked like an abandoned toy lying on the ground we should give it a wide berth and run and tell a grown-up. There was a prisoner-of-war camp near where we lived, and there was some talk that prisoners might escape and plant booby-trapped toys where unsuspecting children would pick them up. I remember being told about this over and over again, but it went clean out of my head the day I saw a shiny red and silver model aeroplane in a hole in a dry-stone wall. I was over the moon as I pulled it out and whizzed it up and down through the air making plane engine noises all the way home.

'Look what I found!' I beamed at Mrs Connop as I walked in the door, holding out my prize.

'You stupid boy!' she yelled, grabbing it from me. 'Do you never listen to anything you're told? How many warnings do you need?'

My mouth fell open. Could it have been a trap planted by a prisoner of war? The thought of the danger I could have been in was chilling, but strangely exciting as well.

When my seventh birthday came round in December 1941, I was hoping that maybe Mrs Connop would buy me a nice shiny plane of my own, but she made a curious announcement one evening.

'Your birthday is too close to Christmas,' she told me, 'so we're going to move it. Your new birthday will be on

February the third. Dennis's is in March and Freddie's is in April, so it makes sense to have them one after the other like that.'

I protested that I'd rather have my birthday sooner than later, but her mind was made up and that was that. I'd have to wait a couple of months to turn seven.

As Christmas approached, we started to get excited about it. We'd never really had a proper Christmas before, although the one on the ward at St Woolos hospital had been nice enough. Mrs Connop and Ginger put up a big Christmas tree in the hall and decorated it with ornaments brought down from the attic. The ones that I was most interested in were little parcels, neatly wrapped up in shiny paper, which hung all over the branches. Every time I walked past I tapped one of them, trying to work out what might be inside and whether any of them might be for me.

The Connops' older children, Michael, John and Olga, came home on leave and Dennis and I pestered them to tell us stories of bombing raids over German army bases, and the Battle of Britain, and what it was really like to pilot a Spitfire. They answered our questions patiently for the most part, only occasionally telling us to 'put a sock in it'.

On Christmas morning we were bursting with excitement when we were invited into the drawing room and handed a parcel each. I could tell straight away that mine wasn't an aeroplane because it was a big flat box that rattled when I picked it up. I tried to smile and look pleased when I opened it to find a board game called Ludo. Freddie got a painting book and some paints and I think Dennis got some books. We were each given a money box shaped like a post box, with a slot to put the coins in and an opening in the bottom where you could take them out. It wasn't exactly what we'd have chosen ourselves, but they were the first Christmas presents we'd ever received and that was a great feeling.

Later that day we had our first proper 'family' Christmas dinner as well: chicken and ham and dried fruit pudding and so much food that we were stuffed to the gills and couldn't have eaten another bite.

Before we went to bed that night, I had another look at the Christmas tree and saw that, intriguingly, none of the parcels hanging on it had been opened. I kept my eye on that tree right through the festive period up to 5 January, when Mrs Connop and Ginger carefully took down all the decorations and packed them away in boxes to go back up to the attic. The next time I could sneak off without being spotted, I climbed the ladder up to the attic and found the box with those parcels in it. I had to know what was inside them. I peeled the paper off the first one and was bitterly disappointed to find it was just an empty cardboard box. I tried another and another until I had opened nearly all the parcels and the floor was strewn with wrapping paper, but they were all merely decorative, with nothing at all inside. It was a bitter disappointment to me.

I'd forgotten all about it by the time my crime was discovered. Some weeks later Mrs Connop had climbed up to the attic to look for something and come upon the bits of Christmas paper strewn about, whereupon she gathered the three of us in the drawing room and urged the culprit to confess. My blushing gave me away yet again, and I took my six of the best reluctantly. That time it definitely hadn't been worth it.

In the New Year of 1942 I began to get friendly with the Connops' lodger, a happy, friendly man whose name I can't remember any more. He walked about the village in all weathers, summer and winter, wearing just an open-necked shirt, short trousers and heavy boots. He always stopped for a chat with any villagers he passed and had a big smile for everyone. At the age of seven, I thought he was an old man but looking back he was probably only in his forties or fifties. One day I admired a pencil that he was using, which was painted gold, and he said I could have it. A real gold pencil! I was over the moon about it and took it to school the next day to show off to all the other kids. It became one of my most prized possessions for a time.

After that, I started hanging around with the lodger when he was working on the farm, asking if I could help out. I liked being with him. He chatted to me as if I were an equal, explaining things about farming and animal behaviour and why you planted certain crops in a field at particular times, and I found it all fascinating.

One day the lodger wanted to saw some small tree trunks that were piled up by the saw bench at the back of the farmhouse, and he asked me if I would give him a hand. The saw bench was a criss-cross wooden contraption. You put a log into the cross-section and then two people were needed to operate the long saw with handles at either end. Although I was only seven, I'd done it before and I knew that I had to push while the lodger was pulling and vice versa.

We'd only just started cutting when all of a sudden the saw blade jumped out of the groove and the lodger yelled in pain and jumped backwards. Blood was gushing from his finger and he sat down hard on a log. I ran inside to get Ginger and I think the district nurse was called out later that evening to have a look at his wound. I felt terrible. It wasn't my fault, but I knew that the cut had been a very bad one.

I don't know if his injury had anything to do with it, but soon afterwards the lodger became very ill. Mrs Connop looked after him herself, bustling in and out of his room with clean bedding and bowls of soapy water and trays with soup and cups of tea. Whenever I peeked in the door he was lying back on his pillows looking gaunt and exhausted and completely different from the cheerful, chatty man he'd been before. He tried to say hello to me but it seemed like a huge effort and after a while I stopped talking to him when I passed and just glanced in timidly at his unmoving shape under the bedcovers.

And then one day Mrs Connop told us that he had passed away. She kept dabbing her eyes with a handkerchief and I could tell that she had really cared about him. People in the village seemed very upset as well and lots of them stopped me to pass on their condolences. 'He was a good man,' they all said.

I felt very sad myself. It was the first time anyone I knew had actually died and while the nuns explained to me that he had gone to Heaven, which was a 'much better place', I found the whole idea that I would never see him again very hard to take on board. 'Never' was such a big word. For ages, I kept glancing into the barn, half-expecting to hear him whistling away in there, or I'd look into his room when I passed and get a shock to see the neatly made bed with no person inside.

And then a few months later, his room was dismantled and a wall removed so that the hallway became much larger than it had been before. No trace of the lodger remained, except for the gold-painted pencil he had given me. That was my first experience of death and for me it was very unsettling and strange.

The year continued, and mostly we were happy-go-lucky kids having an idyllic time. Freddie had joined Dennis and me at school and he was old enough to take part in more of our after-school games. We built a den together in the corner of the chicken shed, where we could hide our birds' egg collection and any other valuables we didn't want grown-ups to find, and where we could stay hidden from Mrs Connop when she was on the warpath. Once we took a baby owl from its nest and carried it to our den, but unfortunately it died as we didn't know how to feed it. Ginger knew about our hiding place but she would never give the game away. She protected us when we got into scrapes, so long as she could do so without getting into trouble herself.

I continued to have a bit of trouble with bullying from some of the village boys. There was one in particular, called Dick, who was the ringleader. He lived in a pink house up at the top of the village along with his nan, to whom he wasn't very nice. I heard him talking to her one day, using all sorts of bad language and berating her: 'I told you to do so-and-so' and then 'Don't argue with me.' He obviously wasn't a decent person. I don't think I was the only person he bullied but I probably used to wind him up a bit. I stood up for myself and didn't take things lying down if someone was mouthing off at me, so I was often in trouble for scrapping. Mrs Connop used to get very cross with me when she found out, but what could I do? I had to defend myself or I would have got hurt.

I also used to get into trouble for being late for school. If I was dawdling around, the others would set off without me and I'd have to make my own way there. One morning in the autumn of 1942, I was ambling along the lane on the outskirts of the village, hitting the heads of dandelions with a stick. I knew I had to get to school but

I was in no particular hurry. Just then a local farmer drove by on his tractor, which was pulling a trailer. I knew he'd be driving up to Croft Castle so I decided to hitch a lift and I jumped onto the back of the trailer.

The farmer turned round and he was not best pleased. 'Oy! You! Get off there!'

I was standing in the middle of the trailer, which was still moving, arms outstretched to keep my balance on the slippery surface.

'Get off before I come back there and drag you off!' he shouted.

I stepped carefully towards the front of the trailer, thinking I could jump off at the towbar, but suddenly my foot slipped. I fell as if in slow motion and hit the ground hard, and the wheels of the trailer trundled over me. The farmer braked abruptly and came running round.

'You stupid idiot! What have you done?'

I lay there, winded, unable to move because I was trapped by the trailer wheels. Fortunately it was empty or it would have been much heavier, but still the farmer had to use all his strength to lift up one side of it so I could roll out, dazed and bleeding.

'Blimey, your knee's in a bad way,' he said, looking down at me.

White bone was visible through a huge L-shaped gash covering my entire kneecap.

'I reckon I'd better give you a lift back home. Connops' place, isn't it?'

'No,' I protested faintly. 'I have to get to school.' All I could think of was that I'd get into trouble with Mrs Connop if she realized I hadn't been in school at that time of the morning.

The farmer lifted me up onto the back of the trailer and drove me slowly through the lodge gates and up the long driveway to the school building. The trailer bumped around causing me a lot of pain, and the journey seemed never-ending. When we got to the school, the farmer explained to one of the nuns what had happened, then carried me inside and sat me down on a chair.

Mrs Connop was phoned to come and get me and, meanwhile, one of the nuns began cleaning and dressing the wound.

'It wasn't my fault,' I told her as soon as the farmer had gone. 'It was his fault for shouting at me to get off the trailer without even stopping it. He was trying to make me hurt myself.'

She ignored me and carried on dabbing at my knee. I couldn't look down at the wound without feeling sick at the sight of all the ripped-open flesh and the blood still oozing out.

Mrs Connop drove me home in her pony and trap, and then called out the district nurse, who took one look and said the wound had to be closed up with metal clips. I don't remember how many she put in because I was almost faint with the pain, but she used a machine like a stapler to insert them right round the wound and then placed a big dressing on top. After she left, I tried to get up and put my weight on the leg but it was agony. All I could do was hop to the kitchen, where Ginger gave me a piece of bread and jam to help me forget about my injury.

I was off school for a couple of weeks and every day that sadistic nurse came round to change my dressing. She was no Florence Nightingale, that one. She'd sit me down on a chair in the hall and rip the bandage off, saying 'This will hurt me more than it will hurt you.' Of course, it was a black lie. Every tug caused stabbing pains that made me cry out loud. She didn't soak the lint with water to loosen it up so the area of bandage that was stuck to the wound pulled off a layer of flesh with it every time.

'Stop with your crying,' she'd say. 'A good tug and the pain will be over quicker.'

Underneath the wound was still jagged and messy and it made me nauseous every time I caught sight of it.

One day the pain was so bad as the nurse tugged at my dressing that I jumped to my feet, slapped her on the face, and hopped down the hall into the kitchen. I was trying to escape but she caught me before I reached the back door.

'What a big baby you are!' she exclaimed, but after that incident she agreed to soak the lint before trying to pull the dressing off, which made things slightly more bearable.

I was a healthy, growing boy, so the wound healed and before long I could run about again, but there was a jagged crimson scar running the length and breadth of my kneecap, which duly impressed the boys at school when I finally got back to show it to them.

'Good one,' said Dennis, running his finger along it almost as if he was jealous he didn't have one as well. 'It's like a war wound.'

The new skin that grew in the area was pink and shiny and over the next few months the scar turned from crimson to purple. It was ugly to look at but I saw it as a sort of badge of courage. Nothing could defeat me now. I was a survivor.

Chapter Five

In the autumn of 1943 Ginger announced she was leaving the Connops'. Over the last two and three-quarter years she'd become a good friend to us, almost like a big sister, and Dennis, Freddie and I were distraught. We ran out to our den in the chicken shed and had a good old cry together. Freddie was particularly inconsolable because she'd become a substitute mother figure for him. He liked to sit on her knee and have a cuddle, and she would always oblige. We weren't ever told why she was leaving. It was just another of those occasions when grown-ups made decisions that affected us and only informed us later.

We watched as she carried her bag down the front path, waving goodbye, and we tried not to cry in front of her. I felt cross with her as well as sad. Why was she leaving us? What reason could possibly be good enough?

'We've got a new maid starting tomorrow,' Mrs Connop said kindly. 'I'm sure she'll take just as good care of you. Don't worry about that.'

But we didn't want a new maid; we wanted Ginger. When the next girl started, we registered our protest by giving her a hard time. We'd play up while she was trying to get us ready for bed, and disappear when our tea was on the table. She had a bad cold when she arrived and was always blowing her nose so I'd chase her round the house calling 'Snotty nose! Snotty nose!' It must have driven the poor girl to distraction. Dennis used to do an imitation of her sneezing that had us in stitches, although he was far too nice to let her see it, as I would have done.

At around this time, Dennis left the Sisters of Charity School, which was just a primary school, and moved up to a Church of England secondary school on the outskirts of Yarpole. I don't think he was very happy there. One day he came home and told Mrs Connop, with barely concealed disgust, that they were having a cookery lesson the next day and he was supposed to bring the ingredients with him.

Freddie and I teased him all night, telling him he was turning into a girl because only girls did cookery.

'Bloody idiots, what d'you know anyway?' he snarled, and we giggled even more.

He set off for school the next day clutching his bag of ingredients and looking rather downcast, but it was a different story when he came home at four o'clock, holding out a golden-brown apple pie. He seemed very proud of it and Mrs Connop said it was a 'perfect piece of baking'. Needless to say, we all helped him to eat it and I have to say it wasn't bad at all.

The problem with Dennis being at another school was that I had no one to stick up for me on the walks to and from school when Dick and the other village bullies started shouting out names or throwing stones at Freddie and me. There were several incidents that came to blows and I was always getting told off by the nuns and, latterly, by Mrs Connop. I didn't think anything of it at the time. Boys had to learn to defend themselves in the world and if you didn't stand up for yourself you'd get walked all over. It was just one of those things. On a couple of occasions I heard Mr and Mrs Connop talking about our 'trouble with the local boys' but frankly I didn't see why they should worry about it. It was up to me to sort it out.

It was in June 1944 that Mr and Mrs Connop called us into the drawing room one night looking very grave. I racked my brains to think of any mischief I'd been up to that they might have found out about, but nothing sprang to mind.

'Boys,' Mrs Connop said, 'we've been aware for some time about the tension between you and some lads in the village. We had to talk to Newport council about it because they have a responsibility for your welfare, and anyway …' She turned to Mr Connop as if looking for back-up. 'A decision has been made that you should go to stay elsewhere.'

'But it's not our fault,' I cried out. 'They've been picking on me all along.'

'That's beside the point. It's all arranged now,' Mrs Connop said. 'A man will be coming to collect you on Wednesday to take you to your new home. I'm sure it will be lovely. We'll miss you, of course, but I know you'll be well taken care of. Lots of people are looking after your best interests.'

We stood frozen to the spot with misery. 'Why can't we stay?' Freddie asked quietly.

'It's for the best,' Mrs Connop said, in a tone of voice that made us understand there was to be no negotiation.

'Why don't we all go and listen to the radio?' Mr Connop suggested. The Allied Forces had landed in France earlier in the month and we'd been following their progress through Normandy, but none of us boys had the stomach for it that night. We felt as if we were being punished for something we hadn't done.

'Life gets tedious, don't it?' Dennis commented drily to me. I didn't know the word 'tedious' but he explained it meant dull or boring. I supposed that was one way of putting it.

In bed that night I asked him, 'What do you think our next place will be like?'

I could almost have predicted the answer, which had become a catchphrase of his: 'If things don't change, they'll stay as they are.'

I decided to be optimistic. Every move so far had taken us somewhere better than the last place. But what could possibly be better than the Connops? I hoped we would be placed on another farm. I liked the farming life, the open fields, the animals and, of course, the access to delicious food when I knew other people were having to put up with rationing. (Mrs Connop was always reminding us that we should be grateful.) I was also going to miss Mr Connop who had been a father figure to me in a way that my own father had never been.

On Wednesday, 28 June 1944, Mr Connop wakened us bright and early and Mrs Connop and the new maid came upstairs to pack our belongings. We didn't own any suitcases so Mrs Connop agreed that she would lend us some so we could take with us all the new clothes we'd been bought during the three years we'd been staying with them. Mr Connop wrapped up our board games and books in brown paper parcels and tied them with string. He was trying to be all jolly but it sounded false and empty and no one was laughing.

I felt an ache in the pit of my stomach. Why did we have to move? I loved staying at the Connops'. Was it my fault for fighting with the local boys? What was I supposed to do when they were bullying me?

We came downstairs for breakfast but I could hardly eat because of the tight feeling in my chest.

'I'll make you sandwiches for the journey,' the new maid said. 'It'll take you a while to get there and you don't want to go hungry.'

It only occurred to me afterwards that she must have known where we were going – something that no one thought to share with us.

At ten o'clock, there was a knock on the front door and a tall man, wearing a brown suit and a trilby hat, was shown into the hall. Mrs Connop came out to shake hands with him.

'They're all packed up and ready,' she said. 'I'll just fetch them for you.'

Dennis, Freddie and I trouped out, our faces tripping us.

'This is Mr Easterby,' we were told. 'He's going to take you to your new home. Be good boys for him and don't cause any trouble.'

Mr Connop shook hands with each of us in turn, wishing us good luck in a gruff voice, and then Mrs Connop gave us each a quick hug.

'Have you got all your things?' she asked. I thought I saw a glint of tears in her eyes but I might have been mistaken. I think she was fond of us, but she was probably looking forward to a more peaceful life once we were gone – me in particular.

Each of us had a small suitcase and our brown paper parcel to carry. We picked them up and Mr Easterby led the way out of the front door and down the path. We caught the bus from Yarpole to Hereford and got out at the stop beside the railway station.

When we realized we were going to our new home by train, Dennis and I looked at each other with barely contained excitement. All those years we'd been watching the trains in the sidings down at Pillgwenlly docks, we'd never actually been on one. We'd seen them puffing along, belching out clouds of steam, pistons chugging in and out of the cylinders, but what would it be like to be a passenger on one, speeding through the countryside?

We climbed the steps and Mr Easterby held the door and ushered us up into a narrow carriage with four seats on either side. He lifted our suitcases into the woven nets hanging from racks above our heads, gesturing for us to sit down. Dennis and I managed to nab the window seats, and Freddie squawked in complaint.

The train puffed away from the platform and we sat mesmerized as the scenery rushed past us. I remember lots of electricity pylons stretching across the fields, and a village called Craven Arms, which made us giggle because it seemed such a silly name. Mr Easterby sat reading a newspaper and not paying any attention to us at all, as we chattered and directed each other's attention to some new sight. He only roused himself to snap at me when I pulled down the carriage window and tried to peer out.

'Sit down, Terence, unless you want your head knocked off when a train comes the other way.'

I jumped back into my seat smartish at that.

The train journey was way too short for my liking – only about an hour – and then we were getting out at Shrewsbury station, from where we had to catch a bus to our destination. There was a long wait before we got onto a trundling country bus that wove its way out of the city, stopping every hundred yards or so for passengers to get on or off. We were starving, so we ate our sandwiches and looked out the windows at the hilly landscape.

'Over that way is Wales,' Mr Easterby gestured, and I gazed out at the dark hills on the horizon, wondering if that's where we were going.

Finally the driver called out 'All passengers for Hope' and Mr Easterby stood up and said 'That's us!' A village called Hope seemed like a good omen.

'I hope we're going to like it in Hope,' I quipped, and Dennis rolled his eyes and said 'Very funny!'

As the bus moved off, we stood by the roadside with our suitcases and packages and Mr Easterby squinted at a sheet of paper on which were written the directions we were to follow. We were standing beside the village shop, which doubled as a post office, and I was aware of some women inside peering out at us with curiosity.

'This way,' Mr Easterby said, pointing across the road. 'Pick up your things and follow me.'

We walked over the road and past the village school. I wondered if this would be the school we were to be sent to and whether I would like it or not. We climbed a steep hill, the road all the while getting narrower. There was a farm near the top called 'White Gates' and, sure enough, I saw the gates were painted white. At a crossroads just beyond, the road split into three and Mr Easterby led us down the narrowest road, which was little more than a dirt track. It was late afternoon by this time and we were all getting tired but there was no sign of human habitation – just a long winding track disappearing off between the trees.

Mr Easterby took off his hat and wiped his brow. 'Not much further now, boys,' he said, and I thought it was all right for him because at least he wasn't carrying a suitcase and a parcel. They weren't heavy but they bumped against our legs awkwardly as we walked.

The track wound its way down a steep hill, and at the bottom there was a metal gate. Were we really at the right place, I wondered? It seemed so isolated, literally miles from anywhere. The track shrank even further until it was just a footpath. We passed a farmhouse on the left and then, finally, another house came into view and Mr Easterby said, with a sigh of relief, that this was the one.

It was a shabby, grey stone house that didn't look very big. I couldn't help thinking that it felt like quite a let-down after the Connops', but I suppose nothing could have been as good as theirs.

Mr Easterby knocked on the door and a grey-haired woman opened it almost immediately.

'Mrs Pickering?' he asked. 'I've brought the Newport boys.'

'Oh, goodness! You'd better come in,' she said, seeming flustered. 'I wasn't expecting you. Here, boys, put your things down in the hall here.'

We marched in and piled up our belongings where she indicated. A little girl, who looked about seven or eight years old, was sitting at the table watching us with a serious expression.

'This is Dorothy,' Mrs Pickering said. 'She arrived earlier today. There's been some kind of mix-up, I think.'

'A mix-up?' Mr Easterby looked exhausted from the walk. He took his hat off and sank into a chair. 'Oh no.' He looked at us. 'Boys, why don't you go and play outside while we try to sort things out. Any chance of a cup of tea, Mrs Pickering?'

I looked at Dennis, who shrugged, and we turned and went out the door again. Behind the house there was a field of tall grass. We could hear the tinkling of water somewhere so we ran through the grass until we came upon a brook, which was about two foot wide, sparkling in the late afternoon sunshine.

'Let's dam it,' Dennis suggested. 'Go and collect all the rocks you can find.'

Freddie and I splashed around collecting rocks while Dennis arranged them across the width of the brook. We didn't talk about whether we would be staying there or what the mix-up might be but the worries were niggling away in my head while we played.

It was about an hour later when Mr Easterby came out and summoned us. He and Mrs Pickering were sitting at the table with the little girl and he introduced us in turn. 'This is Dennis, who's eleven; Terence, who's nine; and Fred, who's seven.' He looked at us. 'Boys, there's a problem in that Mrs Pickering was originally going to take the three of you but now that young Dorothy here has arrived, she doesn't have the room. She can take two of you, but not three.'

We looked at each other in horror. My chest felt tight with a panicky feeling. 'But we have to stick together,' Dennis said.

'I understand that, boys,' Mr Easterby said. 'That's what the Newport authorities want as well, but we're in a bit of a bind because there's no time to find you somewhere else tonight. What Mrs Pickering suggests is that Terence and Fred stay here and I take Dennis to one of the farms up the road. He'll be really close by.'

I shouted out 'No! You can't do that.'

Mrs Pickering rushed to reassure us. 'It'll just be for sleeping. You can see each other during the daytime. Dennis can come down here. He'll only be a few minutes away.'

'I'm afraid it's the only solution, boys. It won't be so bad. You'll see.'

I looked at Dennis and his eyes were wide with anxiety but he didn't say anything more. It seemed the decision had been made.

'You can't,' I argued, but with less conviction because I could tell that nothing I said was going to change their decision. 'Where would you take him anyway?'

'Do you remember that farm we passed called White Gates?' Mr Easterby asked. 'Mrs Pickering thinks they might take him in.'

I nodded, eyes to the ground and a big lump in my throat. Dennis had always been there, all my life, and I couldn't imagine how I would cope without him. Tears were pricking my eyes but I knew I was too old to cry so I held them back. This was the worst thing ever. Worse than leaving the Connops. Worse than being hit by the staff at Stow Hill.

I watched as Dennis picked up his suitcase and brown paper parcel and followed Mr Easterby up the path. He turned once and caught my eye just before they went round a bend that took them out of sight. I hugged myself, feeling very lonely and vulnerable. Anything could happen now and I'd have to deal with it because I was older than Freddie. I had to be the responsible one. But I didn't feel responsible. I felt very young and very scared.

Mrs Pickering made us fried eggs with bread and butter and a cup of tea and tried to chat to us as we ate, but I couldn't speak because of the lump in my throat. Freddie answered her questions in his high-pitched babyish voice and I stayed quiet. We went to bed soon after our meal, but I couldn't get to sleep. It was high summer and still light outside, so I lay going over everything in my head. Why couldn't we have stayed at the Connops? We'd been happy there and I'd thought that's where we would stay until we left home. Now we'd been dumped in a place that seemed a bit rundown and scruffy and much smaller than the Connops, and worst of all we'd been separated for the first time ever. I remembered how upset I had been when Dennis started school six years earlier and couldn't spend the days playing with me, but this was incomparably more awful. I needed the comfort of him being there when I closed my eyes at night. If I woke in the early hours, I needed to hear his breathing before I could go back to sleep again. What would I do without him?

Next morning, we got up bright and early and were eating our breakfast downstairs when Dennis appeared. Mrs Pickering invited him in.

'So are you staying at White Gates then, dear?' she asked.

'No,' he replied. 'They couldn't take me because the lady is expecting a baby soon and they said they've got their hands full. They suggested we tried some people called the Goughs, at Bank Farm. It was quite a bit further on but when we got there they said they'd take me.'

'The Goughs, eh?' Mrs Pickering said. 'I've never been up there. Does it seem all right?'

'I like being on a farm, ma'am,' he replied.

'Well, that's just fine, then,' she said. 'You come down here to see your brothers whenever you like.'

After breakfast, we ran outside back down to the brook and I was delighted just to be by Dennis's side again, hearing his voice, looking at him. It made me feel safe. We found that our dam had held up overnight, creating a nice pool above it where we could paddle. When we explored further, we came across a small wood with some cottages on the other side. A kind lady who lived in one of them gave us a biscuit each, which was very welcome. There were cows grazing in a field and we fed them handfuls of grass, then stroked their heads through the bars of the gate. The lump in my chest was softening slightly. Maybe it was going to be all right here after all. So long as we spent our days together, surely it didn't matter too much if we spent the nights in different places? It was only for sleeping, after all.

A couple of days later, Dennis took me over to see the Goughs' place for the first time. It was a long walk, right the way back past the school and the village store where we'd got off the bus and then along the main road to a five-barred gate opposite a petrol station. After that you had to follow a footpath through a field up to the house, which was fronted by a vegetable garden.

'So this is Terence!' Mrs Gough exclaimed, coming out of the house to say hello. 'Welcome to Bank Farm.'

My first impression was that they must be very poor people because her clothes were worn and faded and her ginger hair was messy like a bird's nest. Mrs Connop had always looked smart, in a skirt and blouse with neatly set hair. Mr Gough came round the corner of a shed and I thought at first he looked a bit scary, with short dark hair, a craggy forehead and bushy eyebrows that gave him a scowling expression, but he greeted me in a very friendly manner.

'You must be missing your big brother,' he said. 'Seems a shame the three of you had to be split up like that.'

I shrugged and looked at the ground. 'You're welcome here whenever you want to see Dennis,' he said. 'Any time.'

His accent was quite different from the Connops': rougher, and with an emphasis on the R's that was like a growl.

Dennis showed me round and I was impressed with all the animals they had: two big horses, lots of cows and some chickens as well.

'I helped to feed them this morning,' Dennis told me proudly, and I was jealous of that. I'd always liked feeding the animals at the Connops'.

The next day when he came to see me at the Pickerings, he said, 'The Goughs have got room for one more and they were wondering if you want to come and stay with them instead?'

I thought about it. 'Nah!' I said. 'I'm fine here.' I felt that I'd only just made a move and Mrs Pickering seemed really nice. I didn't fancy having to move again, even if it meant I would be with Dennis. 'Why don't they take Freddie instead?'

'They said they wanted you. They said they were going to speak to the authorities about it.'

'Is it OK up there?' I asked.

'Yeah, it's fine.'

'Well, we'll see what happens,' I said gloomily. It wouldn't be up to me then. Grown-ups would make the decision for me, as usual.

And that's the way it turned out. On 5 July, just over a week after we'd arrived in the village of Hope, Mr Gough came over to pick me up and take me back to Bank Farm to move in with them. Mrs Pickering was happy about it, so long as she got to keep Freddie as company for the little girl Dorothy.

Freddie looked a bit upset when I picked up my case to go, but he didn't kick off too much because he was already getting quite fond of Mrs Pickering. Besides, Dennis and I had promised we'd come back and visit him most days.

Mr Gough carried my case for me as we climbed up the path to the road.

'We're supposed to send our empty cases back to the Connops,' I told him. 'They're just on loan.'

'I've got an idea,' he said. 'Why don't we fill them full of frogs then send them back?'

I couldn't help but giggle at the thought of Mrs Connop opening a suitcase full of frogs in that grand, oak-panelled hallway and them leaping out all over the place.

'That's what we'll do then,' he said, chuckling. 'I'll see to it later.'

When we arrived, Mrs Gough came rushing out to welcome me and she put her arms round me and kissed me on the cheek. 'Welcome to Bank Farm, dear,' she said. 'I'm sure you'll be very happy here.'

Dennis gave me a wink. I blushed and mumbled 'Thanks' as I pulled away from her embrace. I wasn't at all keen on people hugging me. It was something girls did, something cissy. I was tough now, I thought. I wasn't a kid any more.

Chapter Six

The farm buildings at Bank Farm were all in a row: the two-storey house, with a vegetable garden right in front of it, then the stables, a milking shed and a chicken shed. As well as keeping animals, Mr Gough had six fields where he grew corn and hay.

'Seventy-two acres,' he told me when I asked him how big it was. 'Only small, but we get by.' He looked at me. 'You interested in farming then?'

'Yes,' I said keenly. 'We used to help round the farm at the Connops.'

'You can help here as well. I'll give you some jobs to see how you get on.'

'What kind of jobs?'

'Depends whether you're good at getting up in the morning. I need someone to feed the animals – but I warn you, they get hungry at the crack of dawn.'

'I can do that,' I said immediately. 'Denny and I will do it.'

He explained the job. First we had to go all the way out to the horses' field, which was on a hillside thick with bracken, and persuade them to come down to the stables for their hay. He told us to stand on orange boxes and climb up to slip a collar over each horse's head so we could lead them down towards the house. As we were to find out, some days it was easy and other days those horses seemed determined to make our lives difficult and they'd canter off across the field at breakneck pace. We'd tear after them, our bare legs, clad only in shorts, getting scratched and scraped on the bracken.

'You're too slow, lads!' Mr Gough said when we eventually got them down. 'Don't be all day about it.'

Next, he showed us how to make a 'woo-hoop' sound to call the cattle for milking. They were docile creatures, much easier to control than the horses. Once you got their attention, they ambled into the milking shed contentedly as if they knew their role in life, and Mr Gough and a man called Bob Smith, who helped out on the farm, would milk them.

Finally we had to go into the chicken shed and scatter the feed on the floor, then collect the eggs from their nesting areas around the outbuildings to take to Mrs Gough in the kitchen. Our feet would be soaking wet from the dew in the fields and our faces bright red from the exertion.

'You're going to have to work faster,' she told us on our first morning. 'It's nearly lunchtime. Breakfast was ages ago.' Then she cackled with laughter because we looked so crestfallen. 'All right then, I'll make an exception just this once. Here you go.'

She buttered four slices of bread and handed us two each. I looked at Dennis. We'd only had bread and butter for tea the night before, and it wasn't even real butter but marg, which I wasn't keen on. You'd think they'd have been able to give us butter with all those cows out there. But I didn't dare say anything and neither did my big brother.

We went down to Mrs Pickering's to play with Freddie after breakfast most days that summer, and she usually gave us a sandwich or a piece of cake for lunch or an afternoon snack to keep us going. When we got back to the Goughs at teatime, though, we'd sit down to another meal of two slices of bread and butter.

After a couple of days of this, I decided it must be because they were so poor. They seemed very down-at-heel. When you looked closely, Mrs Gough had sores on her legs, beneath her sagging stockings, just as we used to have when we lived back in Bolt Street in Newport. She never brushed her bushy red hair or put any makeup on her freckly skin. She wore the same clothes day in, day out, as did Mr Gough. His hair was in tight wiry curls when you looked close up and he had a bad smell about him. I couldn't help wrinkling my nose when he stood close to me.

Dennis and I decided that if we wanted more to eat, we'd have to try and make some money ourselves. We passed some crab apple trees on the way down to see Freddie and one day we picked a couple of pockets-full and stopped in at the village store, where we showed them to the storekeeper. She agreed she'd buy them from us, and gave us a few pennies for that first batch. Next day we came back with more of the red and orange fruits, and every day while the crop lasted we did the same until we had earned a few shillings. After the crab apples ran out we picked blackberries from the hedgerows and sold them instead. We spent some of our money on sweets, but the rest we saved in an old red OXO tin that we kept hidden in the bedroom we shared at the Goughs. I didn't tell Mrs Gough about our little business venture in case she wanted to take any of the money. It was ours, fair and square, I reasoned.

A week after I went to live at Bank Farm, there were some new arrivals. A man came from the Shrewsbury authorities bringing a little girl who was only two, and her brother aged four.

'Aren't they the sweetest children?' Mrs Gough cooed, taking the little girl on her knee and bouncing her up and down.

'We didn't realize you had two of the O'Neill children,' the man from the authorities said. 'Are you sure you have enough room? Where are the Mullinder children going to sleep?'

'I'll move Dennis and Terry up to the spare bedroom so the little ones can stay close to me. That's not a problem.'

I looked at Dennis and raised an eyebrow. What spare room did she mean? We found out after the official left when she showed us up a back staircase. The first room we came to had onions spread out drying all over the floor, and then there was another flight of stairs leading to a room with a straw mattress in the middle but nothing else.

'You'll be fine in here,' she said. 'I'll just get you a sheet and a blanket.'

It smelled strongly of onions and there was a thick layer of dust on the floor, no curtains on the window and a general air of neglect. It didn't feel like a bedroom at all – more like a dirty old storeroom – but it seemed we didn't have any choice in the matter.

Any resentment we might have felt towards the new arrivals disappeared at tea that evening when I watched them, close to tears as they munched their slices of bread and marg. The little boy had something wrong with his mouth. It didn't close properly so when he was chewing, crumbs would spray out, and swallowing seemed to be a real struggle for him. The little girl looked tearful and terrified, and my heart went out to them both. It was hard enough to be taken away from their family at such a young age, but they hadn't exactly landed in the lap of luxury with the Goughs.

'Look at the crumbs you're dropping,' Mr Gough chided the boy. 'You mustn't waste food. There's a war on, you know.'

I wanted to speak up for him, to say that it was obvious he couldn't help it, but I didn't like to interfere so we continued to eat in silence. That night Dennis and I arranged a sheet and an old patchwork bedcover over the straw mattress in the spare room. It was scratchy and smelled of onions but we slept just fine, tired out from the exertions of the day.

Sometimes after we went to bed, we heard the Goughs arguing downstairs, but I couldn't make out what it was about. I just heard the raised voices and occasionally a door was slammed, but next morning at breakfast, they'd be sitting as normal, no hint of what had gone on the night before.

After breakfast Dennis and I collected Freddie from Mrs Pickering's and if it was hot we'd all go up to the churchyard in the village, where a fast-flowing brook had been dammed by some local children to make a pool that you could cool off in. At other times we hung around at the Goughs', helping on the farm or playing with the little Mullinder children.

One day Mr Gough took us fishing and showed us how to tickle river trout by rubbing a finger on their underbellies so they went all languid and dreamy. He'd then flick them out of the water onto the bank and finish them off with a sharp blow to the head with a rock. I had a go at it myself but I couldn't get the fish to stay still while I tickled them, and Dennis didn't have much success either. Mr Gough caught four trout that day, and we had a taste of them for tea that night, along with a piece of bread and marg.

A couple of times Bob Smith took us rabbiting in the spinney behind the house. He was a scruffy, unkempt man, who lived alone and survived by doing odd jobs for people like the Goughs. He looked like a tramp and spoke in a rough, country way that was hard to make out sometimes. His method of rabbiting was to put nets over all the exits to a rabbit warren and then send his pet ferret down one of them, so the petrified rabbits hurtled out and either got caught in the nets, where Bob finished them off with a sharp blow to the back of the neck, or they were brought out hanging limp in the ferret's mouth. Our job was to keep an eye on the nets. It was a vicious, bloodthirsty thing to watch the rabbits' sheer terror as they struggled desperately to escape, and part of me was always secretly pleased when one did manage to find a way to freedom. On the other hand, Mrs Gough made rabbit stew one night and it was delicious. I tried not to think about the poor bunnies as I gobbled it down.

When it was raining one day, Mrs Gough taught us how to make rag rugs. We took an old piece of sacking and pulled loops of coloured fabric through from the back with a hook. It was quite fun, trying to get nice colours next to each other, but I wouldn't have wanted to do that every day of the week. It was girls' work, as far as I was concerned.

Once Mr Gough produced a ball and we all went outside to play football – Mr and Mrs Gough, Dennis and me and the two little Mullinder children. It was a perfect, late-summer day and everyone was laughing and happy, trying to kick that ball between the makeshift goalposts at either end of the field. I don't know what happened, but suddenly there was a commotion and the little girl cried out to Mr Gough: 'I don't like you. I'm running away.' And she set off as fast as her tiny legs would carry her – which wasn't very fast.

Mr Gough waited until she got down to the bottom of the field, then he sprinted after her and when he caught up with her, he started smacking her bottom. She screamed in pain and shock and I felt awful. Two years old was far too young to be smacked. Dennis and I looked at each other, wondering if we should say or do something to try and make him stop, but we didn't know what we could say. Mrs Gough was watching impassively and the Mullinder boy looked terrified. It was a horrible sight to see a big man bending over a tiny little girl like that. Fortunately she was still wearing nappies so that would have protected her a bit, but he hit her quite hard, I thought.

Afterwards, when we came in for tea, her eyes were all red and she was breathing in short little gasps. I wanted to say something to comfort her but I couldn't think of the right words so I tickled her instead and she gave me a wan smile.

Mr Gough was in a bad mood that teatime and he started yelling at the boy about spitting out crumbs.

'I've told you before; I will not have food wasted in this house. Get down and pick up every single crumb you've dropped.'

The petrified boy obeyed, picking them up from the muddy kitchen floor, which had been tramped over by our boots with goodness-knows-what on the soles, and putting them back on the side of his plate.

'Now eat them!' Mr Gough commanded, and the little boy had no choice but to obey.

I kept my eyes on my lap because I didn't want to get a telling-off myself. We were finding out that he was an unpredictable man, who could switch from laughing and joking to shouting with rage in a split second. He had only shouted at Dennis and me a few times, usually when we were slow in bringing the animals down in the morning, but there was an edge to his temper that made me nervous around him. He could be play boxing with us one minute and shouting his head off the next, and it meant you could never relax around him.

Sometimes he would say things in a jokey voice but you could tell that he was serious about it. For example, Mrs Gough used to ruffle my hair and give me a kiss on the cheek, and Mr Gough would say 'Is that your new boyfriend then? You trying to make me jealous?' It sounded like a joke – I was only nine years old, for goodness sake – but I could tell he didn't like it when she kissed me. It bothered him. I tried to stay out of her reach if he was in the room so she wouldn't touch me, which seemed like the easiest solution.

Mr Gough obviously had a lot of worries on his mind to do with the farm. One of the calves died that summer, and he was yelling at everyone, blaming them, furious about the loss.

'I saw you hitting that calf with a stick yesterday,' he told me. 'That's probably what killed it.'

I felt awful about it, but when I talked to Dennis he said that Mr Gough had told him to use a stick to make them hurry up when we were taking them to the shed.

'He always hits them much harder than we ever do. I don't think that's what caused it to die,' he said. He thought for a minute. 'It's that drop when they get into the barn. None of them like that.'

There was a step down just inside the barn door, and the calves often stumbled and sometimes fell as we herded them over it. Maybe the calf that died had broken its leg? We had no way of knowing. I'm sure a vet wasn't called out. I never saw a vet all the time I was there.

A couple of chickens died shortly afterwards, and Mrs Gough had a talk with us. 'You haven't been kicking those chickens, have you?' she asked.

Dennis and I both said we hadn't.

'They're only little things. One kick from big lads like you could finish them off. It breaks my heart to see animals and fowl die through neglect, so make sure you take good care of them. Don't let us down.'

I thought back, wondering if I might inadvertently have kicked a chicken at some point, maybe just to get it out of my way, but I didn't think I had. I nudged them with my foot sometimes so I could get past, but I'd never have kicked them in a manner that could actually hurt them. I loved working with the animals and took my responsibilities seriously.

One morning towards the end of the summer, we were sitting at breakfast when Mr Gough jumped up with a loud yell and ran out of the kitchen, knocking over a chair in his haste. We all followed, and a shocking sight met our eyes. There was a big field of golden corn, ripe and ready, that I knew Mr Gough had been planning on harvesting in the next couple of days. However, some cows from the farm next door had broken through a boundary fence and trampled his corn to the ground. They must have been in there for some time because the crop was more or less completely flattened.

We ran out into the field waving our arms and shouting until we had managed to chase the cows back through the gap in the fence. Mrs Gough found some rope and wound it round the fence posts to make a temporary repair, but Mr Gough collapsed on the ground and started sobbing. He put his face in his hands and cried as though his heart was breaking. It was disturbing to watch a grown man in that kind of state and I guessed he wouldn't want us to see him like that so I nudged Dennis and we made our way back indoors to finish our breakfast.

'I feel sorry for him,' I said, 'But a grown man shouldn't cry like that.'

'These things happen when you're a farmer,' Dennis said. 'Goes with the territory. He needs to get a grip on himself.'

At the beginning of September, Dennis and I were due to start attending the village school but something happened in that last week of the holidays that marked the end of the summer for us. We went up to the pond in the churchyard for a dip one day and I'd started to strip down to my underpants when all of a sudden Dennis yelled out in horror and I turned to look where he was pointing. A black and white dog was floating in the water; its four paws tied together, its eyes glassy and staring. Someone had deliberately drowned it. The shock I felt was like a punch in the gut. What kind of person would do that to a defenceless animal? Why? What was in it for them?

It was the first time in my life that I realized what the word 'evil' means and I felt a twisting in my belly. Mr Gough had accused us of killing his calf and chickens and the thought that maybe I had hit or kicked them too hard made me feel sick to my stomach. I couldn't bear to think

I might have been accidentally responsible for a creature's death. But this was different: someone had deliberately grabbed this dog and held it down as they tied rope around its paws, and then they had picked it up and hurled it into the water.

I wished I was brave enough to go in the water and haul it out so we could give it a decent burial, but I wasn't. We were so sickened that we ran away and never went in the pond again, even after the dog had been removed. I felt the water might be polluted in some way. Lying in bed at night, I kept seeing the dog in my mind's eye and thinking about what it had gone through in its last moments of life, and shivered to think that I lived in the same area as someone who was capable of doing that to another living creature. I knew I would look at all our neighbours differently from then on. You couldn't tell who you could trust.

Chapter Seven

Hope Church of England School was a tiny place with only three small classrooms and an annexe, but it had sixty-three pupils ranging in age from five to fourteen. The numbers were swollen because as well as local kids there were evacuees from the cities, sent there to escape German bombs. We already knew some of the children to say hello to as we'd met them by the pond over the summer. On our first day, I kept looking round at the other kids and wondering who could have drowned that poor dog. Was it one of them? Were we in the presence of a murderer? Or could it have been a grown-up? People might pretend to be friendly, but inside they could have the heart of a killer.

The classrooms in that school had big old wooden desks with chairs attached so you had to slide in at the side. There was a hole in the top for the inkpots to go in, and we took turns to fill them up in the morning before class. You could lift up the lid of the desk and keep your jotter inside, along with any food you had brought for your lunch. Mrs Gough gave us each our two slices of bread and marg for lunch every day, wrapped up in brown paper, but I noticed some of the other kids had really nice sandwiches with egg and cress or cheese and pickle, or a slice of cold meat pie.

Once school started, the Goughs allocated more jobs for us to do on the farm, both before and after lessons. As well as bringing the horses and cows in from the field, feeding them and collecting the eggs from the chickens, we now had to clean out the cowshed and sweep the yard, and as the nights got colder we were often sent to collect firewood from the surrounding countryside. What used to be a game quickly became exhausting work. The shoes we had brought with us wore out from the amount of tramping we did across the uneven fields and the Goughs gave us some wooden clogs to wear instead. They were more hardwearing but they rubbed my feet and gave me painful blisters. The autumn was very wet that year and we'd get back to the farm soaked to the skin, bedraggled and bleeding from our blisters or the bracken scratches on our legs, but we didn't get any food until all our tasks were done. That was the rule.

'I'm not feeding you if you haven't earned it, you lazy so-and-so's,' Mrs Gough would say when I asked if I could have half a slice of bread to keep me going.

'Ugly bitch!' I remarked to Dennis once we were out of earshot and he made me laugh by doing an impression of her, hands on hips, saying 'There's a war on, don't you know.'

When we got home from school on 17 October, we were surprised to find the Mullinder children had been taken away. We heard from a friend of ours that a social worker had come from the Shrewsbury authorities and had had a look around the house and said it wasn't suitable for young children to be staying in. I can't say we disagreed with that. It wasn't exactly a palace.

We'd been shunted around so much in our young lives that it didn't seem unnatural to us that foster children could be there one minute and moved somewhere else the next. That's what was always happening to us. We hadn't spent enough time with the Mullinder children to get close to them, so I wasn't unduly bothered. I did wonder if we would get our old bedroom back but it was never mentioned and I didn't like to ask, so we stayed where we were, on the straw mattress in the onion-smelling room.

A social worker came to talk to us at school one day. We sat with her in an empty classroom as she asked us questions about what it was like at the Goughs.

'Are you happy there?' she asked.

'I like working on the farm,' Dennis said, and I nodded in agreement.

'Is the food all right?' she asked, and I hesitated. We were always hungry those days, but it wasn't long after that field of corn had been destroyed by the neighbour's cows and we knew it had cost Mr Gough a lot of money. He probably couldn't afford to feed us more than the bread and marg we were getting.

'I suppose,' Dennis said, noncommittally.

'What do you do in your spare time?' she asked.

I answered this one. 'We help with the animals, and sometimes I help Mrs Gough to make rugs.'

She was writing notes all the time we spoke, only glancing up at us occasionally.

'So you're quite happy to stay there?' she asked at last.

'Yeah,' Dennis shrugged. 'Why not?'

I nodded in agreement again. I didn't want to make another move so soon after we had arrived – unless it was back to the Connops', which would have been wonderful but didn't seem very likely.

The social worker interviewed Freddie after us, and he said he was happy at the Pickerings'. I'd noticed that Mrs Pickering seemed to have a real soft spot for him and I don't think he missed Dennis and me at all. We saw less and less of him that autumn.

Mr Gough's mood seemed to get darker as the days shortened. One day when we were working in the yard, he was driving the horse-drawn grass cutter round a field when the cast-iron seat he'd been sitting on sheared off and he fell into the mechanism. Dennis and I ran as fast as we could to catch hold of the horse before it could walk on and risk cutting him on the sharp blades. He was in a furious mood as he stood up, bruised but not seriously hurt, and that evening he yelled at us and at Mrs Gough, finding fault with everything we did.

'You boys are always messing around and never get your work done on time. Farming's not a game, you know.'

We nodded, agreeing that it wasn't.

'I'm giving you a good training here in how to run a farm and you should be grateful to me instead of always complaining that your feet hurt or you're tired or you're going to be late for school.'

We hardly ever complained, so this wasn't very fair but we both decided not to argue given the aggressive look on his face.

When Mrs Gough served his cup of tea, he said it wasn't hot enough, and the yolk of his egg was too runny.

'I'll have it if you don't want it,' I thought to myself, looking enviously across the table, but I was too nervous to say it out loud. Dennis and I never got eggs or meat. It was bread and marg for every single meal now.

The main thing that made us late for school in the morning was if the horses were being too frisky and we ended up chasing them halfway across the moor before we could get their collars on. One day when we brought them down, Mr Gough flew into a rage with them. He dragged them into the stable, picked up a pitchfork and went in after them, closing the half-door at the top behind him.

Dennis and I stood outside and we couldn't see what was happening but we heard the horses whinnying in terror, a kind of unearthly screaming sound that made the goosebumps stand up on our skin. What on earth was he doing to them?

Mr Gough opened the stable door and walked out a few minutes later, and we saw blood glistening on the prongs of the pitchfork. He marched off round the corner and when we peeped into the stable we saw the poor horses cowering, with nasty wounds scored on their backs and blood spattered all over the stable floor. I couldn't believe my eyes. Many a morning I'd cursed these horses as we ran around after them but I wouldn't have hurt a hair on their heads and I didn't see how Mr Gough could have done it. They were lovely, gentle creatures for all their high spirits, and would have been quite defenceless against his pitchfork.

'How could he?' I breathed.

'He's a bloody maniac,' Dennis said angrily.

My attitude to Mr Gough changed at that point and I became scared of what he was capable of doing when his temper was roused. We didn't have long to wait before it was turned on us again. Just a couple of days later, another calf died and this time he made up his mind it was our fault.

'I saw you hitting it with a stick the other morning when you were trying to get it into the shed,' he said. 'Both of you had sticks and you were being right rough with the calves.'

'I was just tapping them,' I said, feeling sick with worry. 'I didn't hurt them.' When they saw that drop inside the cowshed they didn't want to go in so I would nudge them with my knee from behind and push their necks and maybe give them a little tap but nothing more.

'It can't go on, boys. I'm giving you some stripes tonight so you learn your lesson. I can't have you being cruel to the animals.'

My heart skipped a beat. I didn't know what stripes were exactly but I could imagine.

'We won't do it again,' I pleaded. 'We won't use a stick any more.'

'It's too late,' he said. 'That'll be six stripes each after tea tonight and if you cross me again today you'll get more added on. Also, I'm taking that money you had in the tin in your bedroom. It's the least you can do to make up for the loss of a calf.'

Dennis and I glanced at each other. 'But that's ours,' I said. 'We earned it.' The OXO fund was the only money we had to buy the odd roll in the village shop when we were starving.

'Yes, and the calf was mine,' he retorted, his eyes narrowing with anger.

'We should have hidden it better so the Goughs couldn't find it,' Dennis remarked when we were on the way to school.

'What are we going to do now?' I asked.

'We'll have to figure out a way of making some more. Get your thinking cap on.'

I glanced around but the leaves were falling and there was no more fruit to be had. We'd have to come up with another idea.

All day I waited, heavy with dread, to find out what these 'stripes' might be and how much they would hurt. Mr Gough seemed almost cheerful as he ate his tea, savouring each bite, but Dennis and I sat in misery, our mouths dry as cardboard.

After the meal, Mr Gough went out to the yard then came back in with a thin, bendy stick, about two feet long and the width of a cigarette. It made a swishing sound as he brought it down through the air in a practice stroke.

'Dennis, you first,' he said. 'Stand in front of me and hold out your hand.'

Dennis put his hand out and turned his head the other way as the stick whistled down onto his palm. He couldn't help crying out in pain as it made contact, and he cradled his hand to his chest.

'Hold it out again,' Mr Gough instructed, and the remainder of the stripes were administered.

My heart was beating so hard I thought I would collapse. It was worse being second and watching Dennis's face screw up with pain, and the way he was flinching each time then wringing his hand in a frantic attempt to stop it stinging.

When my turn came, it was hard not to pull my hand away as the stick came towards it but I managed to hold still and just gasped at the burning pain, followed by a throbbing sensation that I could feel right up my arm.

After I'd had my six stripes we were sent up to bed, where we compared the crimson weals on our palms and blew on them to try and take some of the heat out of the wounds.

'Behave yourselves in future, boys,' Mr Gough had said as he finished, 'and there should be no need for me ever to do this again.'

'Christ, that was bleeding agony,' I whispered to Dennis in bed later. 'That was worse than Stow Hill and Mrs Connop and the nuns all put together.'

'I know. I reckon we should be careful we don't get on his bad side any more.'

But the very next morning I accidentally dropped an egg as I lifted it out of a nesting box. I tried to clear up the mess before anyone saw but Mrs Gough came round the corner and spotted it.

'That'll be six stripes for you tonight when I tell the mister,' she said, shaking her head. 'We can't afford for you to be throwing good eggs away.'

All day at school, I sat with a knot in the pit of my stomach, knowing what I was going home to face. After tea, Mr Gough got the stick and I received my stripes, on the other hand this time.

From then on, I think Dennis and I were given stripes virtually every night. There was always something wrong with our work: too slow, too messy, not enough firewood on the pile, mud trampled into the house or, worst of all, more dead chickens. If we committed more than one offence during the day, the totals would be added up over tea when Mr and Mrs Gough compared notes about our behaviour, but it was always Mr Gough who administered the stripes after we'd eaten, a time of day we dreaded deeply.

After he'd finished, we had to say a prayer: 'May God bless us and let us stay here.'

'Thanks a lot, God,' Dennis whispered once we were upstairs. 'I really wanted to live in a house where I got thrashed every night.'

His expression looked grim in the fading light and I shivered.

That autumn the Goughs' attitude towards us seemed to change from friendly and joking to exasperated and then to constantly enraged.

'I thought we were taking on young boys who would help us on the farm but you two are worthless,' Mr Gough berated us. 'Dennis, you are nearly at an age to leave school but I wouldn't employ you for all the tea in China. You're lazy and slow and not even as strong as your kid brother.'

Dennis was still only twelve but the Goughs always seemed to be under the impression he was a year older.

'And you, Terence, are a cheeky so-and-so with a nasty habit of telling lies. Someone needs to teach you a good lesson.'

Nothing we did was right, no matter how hard we tried. I did tell lies – it was true – but only in an attempt to avoid getting punished. Every night there would be more and more stripes, and Mr Gough got a kind of gleam in his eye as all our scores for the day were added together. I think he looked forward to administering our punishments. I actually think he enjoyed it. Afterwards, he would sit in a big chair by the fire, listening to music on the gramophone and looking relaxed and content, his work for the day all done, while Mrs Gough sat opposite making her rag rugs.

At school, we were asked to write essays describing our parents. It didn't occur to me to write about my real mam and dad because all I could remember about them was that Mam had a funny eye and Dad had been a soldier in the war. I'd have to write about the Goughs. It felt strange calling them 'Mum' and 'Dad' in the essays because we never called them that in real life, but I didn't know who else to write about when the teacher gave us the essay topic, and Dennis came to the same decision.

I knew instinctively that I would be in huge trouble if I told the truth about the way the Goughs were treating us: the lack of food, the scratchy straw mattress, the heavy workload and the stripes every night. Instead I wrote: 'My mother is very good and kind to me, she buys me new clothes and new boots and clogs, she lets me make rugs, and I sometimes go to town with her, she sometimes gives me money for working, she gives me lots to eat, and lots of cake, she lets me feed the fowls and ducks and feed the ferrets, and the dog, she gives me sweets and pears, and I get some oranges.'

I had tears in my eyes as I wrote because these were all the things I really wanted in life: cake, sweets, fruit, new clothes and kindness.

Dennis's essay had a few more clues about the way we were being treated, if any teacher had cared to read between the lines. About Mrs Gough, he wrote 'Mum likes me to be quick with the jobs but I must do them properly and she does not like to neglect things. It breaks her heart to see animals and fowl die through neglect.' About Mr Gough, he said 'Dad simply hates anyone telling lies ... he does not like pulling swedes ... he likes to have pride in everything he feeds and everything he does.'

An insightful teacher might have thought to ask him questions about the negative images he painted, but no one did.

I once mentioned to a teacher that the reason I was often late for school was because of all the work I had to do on the farm and I think she said something to Mrs Gough about it, because I got a furious thrashing that night.

'Don't you be telling other people our business,' Mr Gough barked, 'or you'll have me to answer to.'

One night at the end of October, around Halloween, Mr Gough played a practical joke on us. After tea, when it was pitch black outside, he ordered us to go to the field on the other side of the vegetable garden to pick up a spade he said he'd left out there. While we were out there, we heard him yelling at us to come back to the house. We opened the garden gate and started to walk up the path when all of a sudden a huge white shape appeared from nowhere, right in our way.

'Oh Christ!' I screamed and darted off in the opposite direction, while Dennis leapt over the carrot patch and ran to the farmhouse door, banging to be let in, shouting 'Help! Quick! Help me!'

When Mrs Gough opened the door, he dashed into the kitchen, shaking like a leaf. I circled round and rushed indoors hot on his heels. We were standing in front of the fire stammering about having seen a ghost when Mr Gough appeared, clutching his sides with laughter and holding a white sheet.

'Got you going there, didn't I? You thought it was a ghost, didn't you?'

For the rest of the evening he kept chuckling at his own practical joke, feeling very pleased with himself, and Dennis and I felt foolish that we had been taken in.

Later, when we were lying in bed, we heard footsteps coming up the stairs towards our room. The door opened and there was a white figure, just like the one we'd seen outside. I assumed it was Mr Gough trying to frighten us again and determined not to fall for the same trick twice, but then I heard his voice shouting up from downstairs.

'Go to sleep, boys! Stop making such a racket!'

Dennis and I screamed anew because if it wasn't Mr Gough under that sheet, who on earth was it? Could it be a real ghost this time?

Once we were well and truly terrified, the sheet was pulled off and the figure of Bob Smith was revealed, laughing every bit as hard as Mr Gough had done earlier. Dennis and I were so shaken up that it was ages before we could get to sleep. As we lay awake we heard the Goughs arguing downstairs. We couldn't hear what they were arguing about but occasionally we heard swearing when one of them raised their voice.

'You bloody bastard,' I heard Mrs Gough yell, and Dennis and I sniggered quietly under the covers.

We heard him shouting 'Bitch!' as well and then there was a prolonged, high-pitched screaming that chilled my blood. What on earth was he doing to her? Was he giving her stripes? We didn't dare get out of bed to go and peek down the stairwell.

Next morning, as she buttered our bread at breakfast, I tried to catch a glimpse of the palms of her hands but couldn't see any redness or swelling. She was holding the knife quite easily, whereas I found it hard to hold a pen at school after a night when the stripes were on my right hand. She didn't look happy though. She was distant, preoccupied and silent. Mr Gough didn't come in for breakfast that day, not before we went to school at any rate.

As we walked through the fields, I felt a bit more cheerful than usual. 'We weren't given any stripes this morning,' I commented. 'If they're cross with each other, maybe it will stop them being cross with us.'

'If things don't change, they'll stay the same,' Dennis commented wryly, his answer to everything.

But the problem was that things did change. As the last leaves fell from the trees and winter crept in, they started changing fast.

Chapter Eight

In mid November the temperature fell sharply and the ground was sparkling with frost when we got up, shivering, to do our morning chores. We still had only the one patchwork cover on our bed and I asked Mrs Gough if we could maybe have another but she said that one should be perfectly adequate and she didn't want to go spoiling us. Dennis and I sometimes had a scuffle in bed if we thought the other one was hogging too much of the cover but we knew to keep the noise down in case Mr Gough came charging up the stairs, stick in hand.

Dennis caught a nasty cold that month and used to keep me awake at night with a hacking cough. One morning, while we were feeding the chickens, he collapsed on the floor of the chicken shed, giving me the fright of my life.

'Denny!' I yelled, crouching down beside him and shaking his arm. 'What are you doing?'

He opened his eyes, looking groggy and confused.

'What happened?' I asked. 'Were you playing a trick on me?'

'I just felt dizzy,' he frowned. 'I'm OK now.'

He got up and carried on with the work, and I put it out of my mind. I sometimes felt a bit dizzy as well, usually when the hunger pangs were worst.

Some mornings, if Dennis's cough was too bad, Mrs Gough let him stay off school and I had to walk down through the frosty fields on my own, bare legs chapped red and blue with the cold. It was absolutely perishing in the mornings before the sun had a chance to take the edge off the chill in the air.

In the colder weather, it got harder to manage on just our few slices of bread. Back in the summer we'd been able to pick fruit from the trees, or buy food with the money from our OXO tin, but that was gone now. Mrs Pickering used to give us a bite to eat when we went over to see Freddie, but we never had time to visit him now because our chores took so long and Mr Gough would have been furious if we didn't come straight home after school. We only saw Freddie in the playground at school and hardly ever talked to him. We were moving in completely different worlds.

What made me cross was that Mr Gough usually got a proper meal in the evening – rabbit stew and potatoes, or eggs and fried bread, or chicken soup – and he'd devour every bite with relish. The smells would make my mouth fill with saliva and my stomach clench into knots.

I'd try to chew my bread and marg slowly, hoping that way it would fill me up more, but by the time we got to bed I was already starving. I began to dream about food: wonderful dreams in which I sat down to a huge banquet heaped with meat and cheese, eggs and bacon, and mashed potatoes with butter on top. But I'd always wake up to the reality of gnawing pains in my belly and the icy darkness of our bedroom.

I never got into trouble at that school, but one day Dennis was hauled up in front of the headmaster for stealing sandwiches from a boy called Oliver. I expect he was starving. He was bigger than me and probably needed more food to keep going because he was forever complaining of hunger.

'I'm bloody starving,' he would moan. 'Aren't you?'

'Go and have one of the cow cakes,' I suggested.

They were square things made of oats that were used to bulk out the cattle feed and they had quite a nice flavour, but they gave you a very dry mouth afterwards. I was always nibbling them when I got a chance.

'I'm not a bloody animal,' he snapped.

Sometimes we'd pinch something from Mrs Gough's pantry when she wasn't looking – but we always seemed to get caught. I think she counted every single slice of bread and every vegetable in that big stone cupboard and she knew instantly when something was missing.

'Young Terence! You've been thieving again. I'll tell the mister to give you extra stripes tonight.'

We tried our best to do all our chores on the farm perfectly, but no matter how hard we worked it was never good enough and every night we'd get more and more stripes. Each petty little thing was an excuse for us to be given another two, or five, or ten stripes. Mr Gough would sit at the table adding up the totals for the day; then he'd announce 'That's fourteen for Dennis and nine to Terence', almost as if they were the football scores or something.

Most nights Mr Gough did the whacking but if he felt tired he'd tell us we had to whack each other. 'Do it properly, mind,' he'd warn, 'or I'll give them to you again when you're finished.'

It felt horrible having to hit Dennis, especially when I knew he was under the weather with his bad cold, but I had no choice. When it was his turn, he had to hit me as well and he'd gaze at me while he did it with such a sad look in his eyes that I had a big lump in my throat.

Mr Gough seemed to like watching us hit each other. It was as if he took out all the frustrations of his life on us. It was quite different from when Mrs Connop used to hit me on the backside with a stick. That hadn't really hurt much. I'd been upset by the humiliation of it more than anything. I knew she never really wanted to do it and certainly didn't enjoy it but felt she had to punish me so I would learn a lesson. Mr Gough, on the other hand, seemed to like inflicting pain.

Once, when we had finished giving each other our stripes for the night because Mr Gough had been 'too tired', he chortled: 'I feel better now, lads. I'm not tired any more, so I can give you your stripes myself.'

He grabbed the stick and gave us the same number of stripes all over again, chuckling to himself all the while. I was enraged about this, but I never dared to speak out. I was never cheeky or naughty at the Goughs' the way I had been at the Connops' because I was too scared of the consequences.

As time went on, cushions of hard skin formed on our hands and the stripes didn't hurt quite so much. What hurt more were the chilblains that we both got on our feet. They started off as itchy red patches that became more and more painful to walk on, then blisters would form on top, which would burst so that the raw flesh rubbed against our shoes and stuck to our socks. These were agony, a real teeth-clenching type of pain.

My teacher saw me limping one day and told me I had to get cream from the doctor to help my feet heal, but when I mentioned it to Mrs Gough she said, 'Who's going to pay for that, then? Was your teacher offering? I suppose not.'

I'd lie in bed at night huddled against the perishing cold, trying to stop the painful areas of my feet rubbing against the mattress, cradling my sore hands and clutching my growling stomach as it cramped with hunger. If only the weather would get warmer, I thought, things would get better. Maybe if we did our jobs perfectly, the Goughs would give us more food. Or perhaps the

Connops would decide they wanted us back. I often thought about the cosy bed and delicious food we'd had there, and all the warm clothes they had bought us, and I felt like crying.

Dennis's chest infection got worse as the weather got colder and he had so many days off school that he was hardly there at all. He didn't come in once during the whole month of December, when we were busy making coloured paper-chain decorations and models of the baby Jesus in his crib and singing Christmas carols.

Mrs Gough visited the school one day to explain to the headmaster that Dennis wasn't able to attend on account of his chilblains. I was called up to see him later, and I was astonished at what he had to say.

'Mrs Gough tells me that your brother is a bad influence on you,' he said. 'She said he's been ill-treating the cows and also that he stole some money from her.'

I was so surprised at this that I didn't respond straight away. It was the first I'd heard about him stealing money, and I didn't believe it because I knew that if he had he'd have bought food with it and given some to me.

'She's worried that you might turn out the same way as him if you don't watch your step. You won't do that, will you?'

I found my tongue. 'He doesn't mistreat the cows. Honest, sir. It's just hard to get them into the milking shed some mornings when they don't want to go and you have to give them a bit of a shove.'

'From what I hear he's been doing a good bit more than that,' the headmaster said fiercely. 'Mrs Gough said she caught him trying to suck milk from a cow's udder one morning. That's just disgusting. We're not animals, you know.'

'He was probably hungry,' I whispered. I was given milk at school every day but Dennis didn't get any now that he didn't come to school any more.

'Well, he should have gone indoors and had his breakfast like any normal person would do. There's no excuse for it.'

My face was burning with confusion as I considered telling the headmaster that some mornings Dennis wasn't allowed to have any breakfast if he hadn't collected enough firewood. He'd be made to stand and watch us having our meal instead. I should have said something, but in my head all I could think of was the number of stripes Mr Gough would give me when he found out and my courage failed.

'Just make sure you are a good boy,' the headmaster finished. 'The Goughs were very kind to take you in and you should be grateful to them.'

'Yes, sir,' I said, before I slunk out of his office, head bowed.

Maybe the teachers were worried about us after all, or maybe it was just a formality, but in mid December the Goughs received a letter saying that a social worker would be coming for a visit on the 20th, which was a Wednesday. I was to stay off school so I'd be there to meet her.

There was a dense fog that day and when we got up, we weren't sure that she would be able to make it because you could hardly see your hand in front of your face, never mind make out the path down to the main road. All the same, Mrs Gough set us to cleaning the floors and polishing the tabletop and stoking the fire so that it was blazing.

'You'll be good boys when the social worker is here, won't you?' she asked us repeatedly, seeming anxious about it, and we assured her that we would.

It was a little after midday when we heard a rap at the door. Mrs Gough opened it to a slim young woman in a brown hat and coat, who identified herself as Miss Edwards from Newport Council.

'You haven't come all the way from Newport on such a terrible morning, have you?' Mrs Gough asked, but the woman explained she'd had other business up this way and wouldn't be stopping long.

'That's a nice fire,' she said, sitting down in Mr Gough's chair. I gasped because I'd never have dared sit there. She held her hands in front of the flames to warm them while Mrs Gough made some tea.

'Hello boys,' she said, turning to us. 'How are you both?'

'OK,' I said. Dennis didn't speak much these days because it could set off a bout of coughing.

She asked how we liked our school and Mrs Gough told her about the nativity scene we had made. I don't know how she knew because I hadn't told her, but maybe the headmaster had mentioned it.

It was then that Miss Edwards commented on how pale Dennis looked, and the dark rings round his eyes. She asked him if he felt OK but he didn't answer until Mrs Gough prompted him, and then he only whispered 'Yes, ma'am', so faintly you could hardly hear him.

'He's the quiet one of the two,' Mrs Gough said quickly. 'Terence is the lively one. He can be a proper little entertainer, has us all in stitches sometimes.' She ruffled my hair and I flinched.

'Is that right, Terence?' Miss Edwards smiled at me. 'You've just had a birthday, haven't you? You're a big boy of ten now.'

'No, not yet,' I said, 'Because the Connops moved my birthday to the third of February.'

'Did they indeed?' Miss Edwards laughed. 'Well, you'll have to celebrate then instead. What do you both want for Christmas?'

We shrugged. We couldn't imagine there would be any Christmas presents that year given the way things were.

'The council will give you seven shillings towards their Christmas presents, Mrs Gough. And there's another two and six for each boy to put in their savings. You do save up your pocket money, don't you, boys? I hope you don't spend it all in the sweet shop.' She smiled, but we just looked blank. What pocket money was she talking about? We'd never received any.

Miss Edwards was looking at Dennis again. 'He seems awfully thin,' she said to Mrs Gough. 'Is he off his food?'

'He hasn't had much of an appetite while he's had the cough, but we'll feed him up over Christmas and get him right as rain again,' she replied.

'I think you should take him to the doctor,' Miss Edwards decided. 'Newport Council will pay the cost so you needn't worry about that.'

'That's kind of you,' said Mrs Gough. 'It can be hard to manage with two growing boys to feed.'

'Call me on the phone and tell me how much the doctor charges and we'll send it with your next payment,' Miss Edwards assured her. 'We wouldn't want you to be out of pocket.'

It was then I first realized that the Goughs got paid to look after us. Before that I'd assumed they were doing it out of the kindness of their hearts. I wondered how much they received. Couldn't it have bought us more in the way of food, and maybe an extra blanket for our bed? Or a woollen coat and boots like some of the children at school had? I used to gaze in envy as they got wrapped up to go home in their snug winter clothing.

Miss Edwards and Mrs Gough chatted to each other over their cups of tea, while Dennis and I stood to the side, not looking at each other, holding our hands behind our backs.

When she was ready to go, Miss Edwards asked us if we were happy there, and neither Dennis nor I had the courage to say no, we weren't, with Mrs Gough glaring across the room at us. We just nodded miserably and watched her pull on her coat, and walk off down the path, turning once to wave back at us.

I had a lump in my throat and I felt like crying as her shape disappeared into the fog. I didn't need to tell her everything but surely if I'd mentioned that we were starving, she would have arranged to get us some more food at least? Surely Newport Council would pay for it? But the beating I'd have had from Mr Gough wouldn't have been worth it. My life wouldn't have been worth living after that.

As soon as she was out of sight, Mrs Gough turned to us. 'Thanks for nothing, boys. You could have been a bit more enthusiastic. The two of you hardly said a word. Who knows what she'll be thinking?' She clattered the visitor's teacup into the sink. 'You were so rude today. That's twenty stripes each tonight. I'll be sure to tell the mister about it.'

She threw us outside to go and help Mr Gough round the farm, despite the freezing fog, and I rounded on Dennis. 'Why didn't you say something to her? You didn't even open your mouth.'

He shrugged and said, 'What's the point? Nothing would change.' His whole posture seemed defeated and I hardly recognized the flat tone of voice he used.

'You're my big brother,' I snapped, exasperated. 'Why don't you act like it for once?'

I felt guilty as soon as the words were out of my mouth because I could tell he didn't have the energy for anything these days. He seemed exhausted the whole time. At least I got some respite from the Goughs when I was at school, but since he had stopped going to lessons he had to put up with their bullying and nagging all day long.

I wondered when Mrs Gough would take Dennis to the doctors, as she'd promised, but when I asked her about it she said the doctor would be too busy with it being Christmas, and we'd wait and see how he was doing after the holidays. I wondered if I'd get a chance to talk to the doctor as well. My chilblains were agony whenever I walked now, and I had weeping sores on my legs just like the ones I'd had back in Bolt Street. I knew I needed some of that brown liquid the nurses used to paint all over me in the hospital back there. The sores were itchy but they hurt when I scratched them. My nose had started running all the time as well, just as it used to when I was little. I never had a handkerchief so I had to blow and pinch off the snot with my fingers. Once I got stripes for wiping my nose on my sleeve, so I didn't do that again.

The school term ended for the holidays and now I was in the same position as Dennis – stuck at home all day being given jobs to do out in the perishing cold. I really missed the school milk, which had helped to line my stomach in the mornings. Sometimes I doubled over with sharp hunger pangs that felt like someone was stabbing me in the gut.

Mr Gough was in a foul temper all the time and our nightly beatings got worse and worse. One night I was given fifty stripes, while Dennis got forty-two, and the next, which was Christmas Eve, we both got a hundred. It took ages for Mr Gough to administer them and I think it made his arm hurt because he kept rubbing his shoulder and swearing. He made us count out loud, while the other one was getting their stripes. Although my palms had been toughened by all the beatings on other nights, they split open during that onslaught and the stick was covered in blood. I was whimpering with pain, just trying to concentrate on the numbers and thinking 'Only thirty to go', 'Only twenty to go'. When he had finished, we ran our hands under the cold tap. I looked at Dennis's and saw they were a bloody mess, just like mine.

On Christmas morning, we had to get up and complete all our chores, just like any other day. My fingers were curled over my palms like claws and they were so stiff and sore that it hurt whenever I had to pick anything up. When we came back it was the usual bread and marg for breakfast, but afterwards Mrs Gough handed us a small parcel each, wrapped up in newspaper.

'Merry Christmas,' she said. 'Hope you like them.'

Dennis and I hesitated, looking at each other. I wondered if they were playing a trick on us, as they had with the 'ghost' at Halloween, and if I would find something horrible inside.

'Go on, open them,' Mr Gough urged.

I opened mine awkwardly, and inside was a pack of playing cards.

'I'll give you a game of rummy this evening,' Mr Gough promised in a falsely jolly voice, 'if you're good boys.'

Dennis opened his package and, glancing over his shoulder, I saw he'd received some cigarette cards. There was a mixture of aeroplanes, ships and football cards in there, so it didn't seem like a complete pack.

'Thank you, sir. Ma'am,' he said, his voice so quiet I had to strain to hear him.

'Yes, thank you,' I said quickly. I couldn't help thinking that they must have got a lot of change from the seven shillings Newport Council had given them to buy us presents. But maybe we'd have a decent Christmas dinner because I'd seen Mr Gough wringing a chicken's neck the day before. That was something to hope for.

My hopes were dashed when teatime came and the usual bread and marg was put on our plates, while Mr and Mrs Gough sat down to a roast chicken dinner with roast potatoes and swedes and carrots and gravy. I felt like crying as I thought of the dinner we'd had at the Connops' the year before, when we stuffed ourselves with so much food we could hardly move afterwards. I wondered what Freddie was having down at Mrs Pickering's? I bet he'd get something delicious there. If only I'd persuaded him to come up to the Goughs' instead of me, then I would probably be sitting down to roast chicken and potatoes just as the Goughs were.

When we got up to bed that night, I asked Dennis if he fancied a game of cards.

'No thanks,' he murmured, already huddled and shivering beneath the bedcover.

'Can I look at your cigarette cards?' I asked.

'Take them if you want,' he said listlessly.

I picked them up and flicked through them for a while in the moonlight shining through the window, then lay back on the pillow. Downstairs Mr Gough had his gramophone on and I could vaguely make out the sound of Bing Crosby singing 'I'm Dreaming of a White Christmas'. I guessed it was meant to be a happy song but for some reason it always brought tears to my eyes. I suppose it was because it made me think about all the things that I dreamed of that never ever happened.

Chapter Nine

The temperature plummeted after Christmas and we had to break the ice on the animals' water troughs each morning so they could have a drink. A few days into January it began to snow and our morning forays to get the horses while wearing only short trousers and wooden clogs became intolerable. My legs would be completely numb and I'd be shaking convulsively by the time we got back to the house. I can still remember the excruciating agony when I stood in front of the fire trying to warm myself afterwards: as the circulation returned to my feet, the chilblains stung badly, making me cry and hop about.

There was no bathtub inside the farmhouse and we used to wash ourselves at the kitchen sink, where there was only a cold tap. One morning, when Mr Gough was in a foul mood, he yelled at Dennis, 'You stink, you dirty little devil. Get outside and have a bath in the water trough.'

Dennis looked petrified and I glanced round at Mrs Gough, hoping that she would intervene. Surely he was joking?

'He's right. You smell like something the cat dragged in,' she said.

I followed them as they frogmarched Dennis out to the yard, hoping against hope that they wouldn't really make him get in the icy water. When would Mr Gough start chuckling and say it was just a joke, like the ghost at Halloween? If he was serious, did that mean it would be my turn next? Dennis broke the ice on the trough and started splashing his face and arms.

'Not like that!' Mr Gough yelled. 'Take your clothes off or you'll never get clean. Hurry up. It's good for the circulation.'

Dennis didn't move at first so Mr Gough charged up to him and started pulling at his jumper. I stood still, transfixed with horror. Surely this was the worst possible thing for Dennis's poorly chest? And then when I saw how skinny he had become, the fear deepened. He was just a bag of bones, his ribs protruding, no flesh left on him at all. I got a real fright seeing him. Was that what I looked like as well? There were no mirrors in the house so it was hard to tell, but I knew my hip bones stuck out in a way that they never used to.

Dennis dipped himself in the water, gasping with the cold, and washed as quickly as he could before pulling his clothes on again over his wet skin and darting back to the kitchen to try and get warm and dry by the fire.

'You next, Terence,' Mr Gough yelled.

Mrs Gough pulled me towards her and sniffed, then kissed the side of my head. 'He's all right,' she said. 'He doesn't smell yet, not like his brother.'

I was off the hook that morning, but the following day I was forced to strip naked and wash in that trough, and it was like millions of needles pricking into my flesh. It gave me a pounding headache and the cold penetrated so deep inside my bones that I couldn't get warm again for the rest of the day.

'I wish I was a chicken,' Dennis said in bed later. 'They get treated much better than us.' It was true: they had food, warm nesting boxes and no cold baths or stripes.

The next day it was Mrs Gough who ordered Dennis to get in the water trough. 'Strip off and have a wash, you disgusting boy,' she ordered him. 'I can smell you a mile off.'

She followed him to the kitchen door.

'Leave your clothes on the water pump so I can check if they need washing,' she said.

He stripped off by the pump and then had to run right across the yard to the trough, break the ice, get into the water up to his neck, then sprint back across the yard again, looking as pale as a skeleton. Mrs Gough hadn't bothered to check his clothes. The only reason I could see that she'd made him leave them on the water pump was so he'd have to run naked across the yard and back. I watched him getting dressed again, still wet, and I knew the fiery pain he was experiencing as the blood flow returned to his limbs. Why were they doing this to us? Why did they choose the coldest days of the year to make us wash outside?

While we were feeding the chickens that morning Dennis passed out again. Mrs Gough came in and saw him lying on the ground. 'You having one of your fits again? Play-acting's more like it. Don't think you're fooling me.'

I knew he wasn't trying to fool anyone – he was starving. He'd had no tea the night before and had been forced to stand and watch us eating. I'd racked my brains trying to think of a way I could save some of my bread and marg for him, maybe by hiding it in my trouser pocket, but I'd have been spotted and they'd have taken it away from me as well. I felt terribly guilty that I had food and he didn't, but wasn't brave enough to stand up for him. God knows what the Goughs would have done.

Dennis was getting very slow in finishing his tasks, and the slower he got, the more enraged Mr Gough became. Every time he saw him, he'd shout at him about something.

'How can you take three hours to collect a bundle of firewood? You could have gone to Shrewsbury and back in that time.'

'Why's there a pile of shit in the cowshed? I should rub your nose in it, I should.'

'Lazy lump! Who said you could have a sit-down when there's work to do?'

There would be more and more stripes, and Mr Gough also started locking Dennis in a cubby-hole by the fireplace as a punishment. It was a cupboard really, easily tall enough to stand up in but only about three foot wide and three foot deep. I watched as Mr Gough screwed a bolt on the front that slid into a groove on the other side, so that it couldn't be opened from the inside. Dennis would be locked in there for an hour or so at a time, and I knew he hated it.

'What's it like?' I whispered to him in bed at night.

'Dark,' he replied.

'Can you hear what's going on outside?'

'Not really.'

I dreaded being put in there myself because I wasn't keen on the dark, or on being confined in small spaces. Dennis often fainted in the cubby-hole, I think, and he blinked for ages after he was let out, as though his eyes were hurting in the light.

If things don't change they stay the same, Dennis had always said, but it seemed to me that every day got worse on Bank Farm that winter. There was no respite. We got more work, more stripes, less food, and it just got colder and colder every day. The Goughs got crosser and crosser, and Dennis and I tiptoed around them, terrified of putting a foot wrong. Every day there was some new rule we had transgressed, or a new crime we had unwittingly committed.

One morning while we were eating breakfast, Mrs Gough was sorting through a laundry pile she had stacked up by the sink. All of a sudden she let out a yell of disgust. 'Which of you mucky boys has made a mess on the sheet? Come over here.' She waved the sheet at us.

I looked and saw there was a tiny brown smear on it, as if one of us had been to the toilet and not wiped our bottom afterwards. I felt a clutching sensation in my chest.

'It wasn't me,' I said quickly.

'It wasn't me either,' Dennis said.

'Well, it was definitely one of you and I want to know which one so you can take your punishment. The mister will be hearing about this.'

Out in the yard, I turned on Dennis. 'It couldn't have been me,' I said. 'I didn't even go to the toilet yesterday.'

'Neither did I,' he replied.

'You must have.' I didn't know whether it had been me or not but I was arguing through fear of the punishment this crime could earn. What if they locked me in the cubby-hole? Or didn't give me any tea? I felt desperately scared, and I suppose Dennis did as well, because suddenly we were tussling with each other.

'Tell her it was you,' he hissed, trying to knock me to the ground. Just a couple of months ago he'd have won easily in a fight, but now he felt much weaker and I managed to stand my ground. He punched me on the side of the head and I hit him on the shoulder.

'It wasn't me. It was you,' I kept repeating.

Unable to vanquish me by any other means, Dennis turned and picked up a shovel that was lying on the ground and swung it at my head. I ducked out of the way and picked up a broom. Gripped with fury, I managed to strike him across the back with it and although I didn't hit very hard, he wobbled on his feet and nearly fell. When he'd regained his balance he came at me waving the shovel again and it hit me on the arm, the cold metal bruising me.

'Stop that, the pair of you!' Mrs Gough yelled from the kitchen door. 'I'll tell the mister later and he'll give you a right good thrashing.'

We stopped at that and looked at each other in dismay.

'Get on with your jobs, now. I don't want to hear another squawk out of you.'

We slunk off to our respective chores, but our troubles for the day weren't over. There was a newborn calf in the cowshed that needed to be handfed. Mrs Gough came out to supervise as I tipped up a bucket of milk to feed it. All of a sudden it reared its head inside the bucket, causing the milk to spill all over the floor.

Mrs Gough went berserk. 'What are you doing, wasting milk like that?' she screamed. 'Can't I trust you with anything today? You useless, good-for-nothing boy! I need you out of my sight.'

She grabbed me by the ear and dragged me back to the house, berating me all the way, telling me that I was stupid, clumsy and lazy, and repeating her threats about the thrashing I'd get later. Once we were inside, I realized she was taking me to the cubby-hole and I cried out 'No, please don't. I'll be good. I promise.'

'It's too late for that,' she said, as she pushed me inside and bolted the door behind me.

It was pitch black, with not even a chink of light coming in the sides. The air felt stuffy and I panicked that I wouldn't be able to breathe.

'Let me out!' I shrieked and pounded on the door with all my strength, but there was just a deathly silence and nothing happened.

I slithered down to sit on the floor with my knees bent up to my chest, my heart pounding. Was I going to suffocate in there? How long would it take? Would she come and free me before then? Then my thoughts turned to the punishment I was going to receive that evening. How many stripes would it be? Would I get any dinner? School was starting again in a few days' time and I prayed I'd be allowed to go back to it, just to get away from the Goughs for a few hours. Over the Christmas holidays I'd been with them the whole time and I felt constantly on edge, terrified about what I would be accused of next. It would be a huge relief to sit in a warm classroom among other children, doing sums or reading from our textbooks.

Time went on and on, and I began to worry that they would leave me there overnight to teach me a lesson. I couldn't bear that thought. Eventually Mrs Gough pulled the door open and I saw Mr Gough sitting at the table with a cup of tea in front of him. His eyes gleamed as he looked at me.

'Been a naughty boy, have you, Terence? Fighting with your brother and spilling milk? You need a right good thrashing tonight, don't you?'

My face flushed hot and my heart was beating so hard I was sure I was going to have a heart attack. It felt as though it could burst right out of my chest with the next beat.

I was forced to stand and watch while Dennis got to have tea that night. He caught my eye and made a sympathetic mouth but there was nothing he could do. After tea, he got his stripes first, then Mr Gough turned on me, his face red and twitching. When I saw the state he'd worked himself into, for a moment I considered turning and running out the door – but where on earth could I run to? I'd die out there in the raw winter cold. I had nowhere else to go.

He beat me on the hands first, putting all his brute strength into each blow, and then, as if that wasn't enough, he started hitting out at my backside and my legs. Tears were rolling down my cheeks, it stung so badly.

'You'd better stop,' Mrs Gough cried. 'He's got school in a couple of days. You don't want …'

She didn't say any more, but after one last whack, Mr Gough was finished. 'Get up to bed and let that be a lesson to you,' he growled.

'You OK?' Dennis asked quietly when we got into bed.

'Yeah,' I said gruffly, turning away because I was embarrassed that he'd seen me crying like a baby.

'Sure?' He patted me on the shoulder.

'Yeah.' It wasn't true, of course. My hands were so sore I couldn't undo the buttons on my trousers, and I had to lie on my front so the straw underneath the sheet wouldn't irritate the weals on my legs.

On 8 January, which was a Monday, we woke up to find it had snowed in the night and everything outside was covered in a blanket of white. It took ages to see to the animals because we had to trudge through the slippery snow. It was several inches deep and came right up over the top of our clogs. By the time we got back to the house for breakfast, we were soaking wet and shivering with cold. But the good thing was that school started that morning and I was praying we would be allowed to go. I couldn't wait to get away from the oppressive atmosphere on the farm.

'The mister has gone to Welshpool with a calf,' Mrs Gough told us over breakfast, 'and I don't want to be on my own here all day, so you'll have to stay behind, Dennis.'

His face fell.

'There's not much to do now the animals are seen to,' I argued on his behalf. 'And the teachers will wonder where he is.' I'd never have dared to argue with Mr Gough but I usually got away with a bit more with her.

'Just tell them he's under the weather,' she said, narrowing her eyes. 'Anyhow, it's not long till he leaves school for good so they won't be that bothered.' She turned to Dennis. 'I need you to go up to the spinney and fetch some firewood. We're running short. Make sure it's dry so it doesn't make the chimney smoke.'

'But it's snowing,' he protested faintly. 'There won't be any dry wood.'

'Are you arguing with me?' she said, with a warning note in her voice. 'Don't think you can take advantage just because the mister's not around. I want a nice big fire in the grate for him when he gets back and you'll make sure I've got the wood for it.'

'I already had a look this morning while we were out and couldn't see any sticks that aren't covered in snow.'

Her temper had been on a knife edge and suddenly she snapped: 'How dare you argue with me? How dare you? After all we've done for you? Get out!' She picked up Mr Gough's stick and ran at him. 'Get out!'

Dennis scuttled out of the door into the yard. Mrs Gough stood in the doorway and threw her wooden clogs after him.

'But I can't walk,' Dennis pleaded. 'My feet hurt too much.'

Mrs Gough rushed out, grabbed him by the hair and dragged him across the yard towards the spinney. 'Don't come back till you've got enough wood for the rest of the day.' She spun round and glared at me where I was watching from the doorway. 'What are you staring at? Get a move on and get out from under my feet.'

When I left for school a few minutes later, I spotted Dennis huddled by the shed, sheltering under the overhanging roof, so I went over. It was then I realized he was crying, and tears came to my eyes. He never cried. It scared me to see him like that. I put an arm round his skinny shoulders.

'What am I going to do?' he sobbed. 'What can I do? There won't be any dry wood.'

'Maybe if you look underneath the bushes in that overgrown bit, there might be something there.'

'My feet hurt so badly.' He was crying so hard that he choked on his words. 'I c-c-can't do it.'

'Maybe Mr Gough will understand. He knows what it's like out here today.' Even as I said it, I knew this wouldn't be true but it was all I could think of to say. I gave his shoulders a quick squeeze then I had to turn and head for school. I was late already.

All day I couldn't concentrate on the work because I was so worried about Dennis. I felt sick with anxiety. If he couldn't cope any more, how would I manage? When I looked out the window, fresh snow was still drifting down from dark grey skies and I knew he'd freeze if he was forced to stay outside in that weather. I prayed he had come upon some firewood somewhere so Mrs Gough had let him back into the house.

When I hurried home at three o'clock it was already dark, and the cold felt threatening, as though it could suck the life out of me. It was a damp, heavy, bitter, all-enveloping cold. I blew on my fingers and stamped my feet, despite the pain of my chilblains, just to keep the circulation going.

When I opened the kitchen door I was relieved to see Dennis inside, sitting at the kitchen table with his head in his hands. Mrs Gough's first words cast me down again, though.

'Your dirty thieving brother has been stealing food,' she yelled, as Dennis quivered in the background. 'I went into the pantry and found him taking a bite out of a swede.'

Oh, poor Dennis, I thought. He was really going to get it later. They went mad when we stole food.

'You boys had better see to the animals before it gets too dark. Off you go,' she chided.

As soon as we were out in the yard, I asked Dennis if he had managed to find any wood and he shook his head miserably. In silence we trudged out to the barns to feed the animals and lock the chickens away for the night. While we were up at the top field with the horses we saw a dark shape coming through the driving snow and go into the kitchen and we knew Mr Gough had come home.

'It's him,' Dennis whispered in dismay. 'I'm for it tonight.'

Neither of us could face him. Despite the freezing temperatures, we took as long as we could over our chores, terrified of what was going to happen when we went into the kitchen.

When we couldn't delay it any longer, I crept in first, with Dennis right behind me. The Goughs were sitting at the table over a cup of tea.

'See!' Mrs Gough cried. 'He hasn't brought any wood. Not so much as a stick. They've been playing me up all day long, with you away. I've been at my wits' end.'

Mr Gough shook his head. 'No tea for either of them tonight, missus. I'll deal with them later.' He turned to us and snapped: 'Stand there and don't move unless I say so.'

We stood stock still, not even daring to glance at each other, while the Goughs had vegetable soup and bread for their tea. I listened to the sounds of them slurping their soup, with the fire crackling behind me, and I felt faint with fear.

When he'd finished eating, Mr Gough stood up and fetched the stick. 'You first, Terence,' he said. 'Come over here.' I didn't know what I was supposed to have done wrong that day and started to say so, but he yelled at me to shut up and began hitting me. He was in a frenzy, completely out of control in a way I'd never seen him before, as though he blamed me personally for everything that was wrong with his life. The pain was horrible and although I tried to be brave at first, by the end I was howling like a baby.

When he'd finished he pushed me away and said, 'Now, Dennis, your crimes are more serious. Stealing food from us and then refusing to fetch firewood when Mrs Gough asked you to are both terrible things. You're going to have to take your clothes off to get your punishment tonight.'

Dennis looked utterly petrified and didn't move.

'Are you going to take them off yourself or will I come and do it for you? Maybe you fancy a bath in the water trough first?'

He chased him out into the pitch-dark yard, and a few minutes' later he came back in holding Dennis's clothes and shut the door behind him.

I was more scared than I'd ever been in my life before. 'Where's Denny?' I whispered. What had he done to him?

'Just making him wait outside for a bit,' Mr Gough said.

In my head I started counting – 'One, two, three, …' – just to try to stay calm. I'd got to over two hundred before Mr Gough opened the back door. As Dennis walked in, naked and shivering hard, Mr Gough drew back his fist and punched him in the face. I jumped with shock, but Dennis just clutched at his nose and staggered backwards.

'Get in the kitchen, you little bastard!' he snapped. 'Bend over the pig bench.'

The pig bench was a hollow stool used for draining pigs' blood after they've been slaughtered. I don't know why they had one when they didn't keep pigs; maybe they used to. Mr Gough pulled it to the middle of the floor and, after glancing round at me with a pale, terrified expression, Dennis bent over it. Mr Gough produced a rope and tied him across the bench, and Dennis started whimpering.

'No, please don't …' His whole body was shaking as he strained against the ropes.

'I'm just doing this to show you what would happen if the police came to arrest you,' Mr Gough said. 'This is what they do to bloody little thieves.'

I wished with all my heart that I was brave enough to kick Mr Gough on the shins, push him over and help Dennis to escape. But I'd never have time to untie the knots before he got up and grabbed me, and then he'd beat me as well. I was too terrorized to do anything but stand and watch in sick horror.

'Terence, get that lantern and bring it here so I can see what I'm doing,' Mr Gough told me.

I lifted down the storm lantern that was suspended from a hook on the wall and carried it slowly over towards the pig bench. Mrs Gough sat at the kitchen table watching impassively. She had no expression on her face at all, which I thought was odd. Mr Gough's face was grim, his jaw set and eyes narrowed.

I held the lamp close by, Mr Gough lifted the stick, and then he brought it down hard on Dennis's naked back. Dennis let out a piercing scream. Tears started to pour down my cheeks. I couldn't help it. I wished with all my heart that I could stop him but there was nothing I could do. Mr Gough hit him again and again and I was crying so much the lamp was shaking, casting shadows that jerked back and forwards around the room.

'Oh, for goodness' sake,' Mr Gough snapped crossly. 'You're no use to me. Put the lantern down and go on up to bed.'

I placed the lantern on the floor and, with one last look at Dennis I turned and climbed the stairs to our bedroom. I took my trousers off and lay on the straw mattress in just my shirt, pulling the cover over me. Downstairs, Dennis was still screaming in agony. I couldn't even count the number of strokes he took that night because it went on for ages. I put my hands over my ears but I was wide awake, looking out the window at the stars, trying to blank everything from my mind.

After a while I realized it had gone quiet but still Dennis didn't come up the stairs. Where could he be? What were they doing to him now? I lay awake, waiting for him, wanting to comfort him when he came up to bed.

It was maybe an hour later when he finally crawled into the room and got into bed beside me and straight away he cuddled up to me to try and get warm. His whole body was like a block of ice and he was just crying and crying.

'It hurts so bad,' he sobbed, and his fingernails dug into my back through my shirt.

'Shh. Keep quiet,' I whispered, trying to prise his nails off me. I could hear the sounds of movement downstairs and was scared of Mr Gough coming up, stick in hand.

But Dennis couldn't stop crying. 'My back! My back!' he wailed.

'Shut up your noise right now or I'll come up there and make you shut up!' Mr Gough yelled up the stairs.

'Dennis, you have to stop crying,' I whispered, in a panic. Mr Gough was completely deranged that evening, and I dreaded to think what he might do next.

Dennis was shaking convulsively and he just couldn't stop the sobs that burst out of him. Every time he made the slightest movement he cried out in agony. It seemed as though every bit of him hurt. He'd never been a cry-baby. I'd known Dennis put up with all sorts of injuries without complaint, so I knew this was bad.

Then I heard Mr Gough's footsteps on the stairs and I went rigid with fear. He burst into the room, pushed me out of the way and rolled Dennis onto his back. With one knee up on the mattress, he raised his fist and punched Dennis hard on the chest. On the mattress beside him I was bounced up and down with the force of the blow.

'Will … you … shut … up!' he yelled.

Dennis started to scream but it was cut off as the breath was knocked out of him. Mr Gough punched him as if he was a punch bag, with all his grown man's strength, over and over again.

When he'd finished, he threatened, 'If there's any more noise I'll be back,' before he turned and stamped his way down the stairs again.

Dennis quietened down after that, biting his lip to stifle the moans, but I could tell he was in horrible pain. I put my arms round him to try and warm him but it hurt him too much when I touched his back. He couldn't get comfortable no matter how he lay and he kept clawing at me with his fingernails, almost as if begging me for help. But what could I do? I was as powerless as he was.

'It'll be all right,' I whispered, very softly. 'It'll be all right.'

The lights went off downstairs and I guessed the Goughs had gone to bed. Still Dennis was making funny little gasping noises, and moaning with pain, but he wasn't crying out any more, and he wasn't talking. I nodded off to sleep for a while but was wakened by Dennis digging his nails deep into me and squeezing tight.

'Get off!' I whispered, and moved his hands away again, then I fell back to sleep.

Chapter Ten

When I opened my eyes the next morning, I could tell from the light outside that we'd slept in. Dawn was breaking, weak sunshine reflecting off the snow-covered ground, and we should have been out there already feeding the animals.

'Dennis,' I whispered, but there was no reply. 'Dennis, we're late.'

I pulled on my socks and trousers, glancing at him, but he appeared to be in a very deep sleep. I leaned over and shook his shoulder. 'Dennis, hurry up or we'll get into more trouble.'

He felt absolutely freezing and his face was pure white, but he looked peaceful and I didn't want to force him awake after his ordeal of the night before so I pulled the cover over him and tucked it in under his chin.

My back felt sore where he'd been clawing at me and when I twisted round I could see he'd scratched me so deeply he'd drawn blood in places. He must have been in unbearable pain to do that. I was worried that if I forced him awake the pain would come back again. At least he couldn't feel it in his sleep.

Maybe if the Goughs had calmed down this morning, I could say that Dennis wasn't feeling very well and they'd let him have a lie in. But I hesitated, scared that they might punish me instead. I knew I couldn't cope if I was tied to the pig bench and thrashed the way I'd seen them thrashing Dennis.

At last I couldn't leave it any longer. With another look at Dennis's still form, I crept down the stairs. Mrs Gough was sitting at the kitchen table having a cup of tea and there was no sign of Mr Gough so I assumed he was outside seeing to the animals.

'Denny's still asleep,' I said. 'I can't wake him.'

She stared at me for a few moments, her eyes wide and startled. 'Are you sure?' She clasped a hand to her mouth then when she spoke again, her tone was surprisingly kind. 'Just let him be for a while,' she said. 'I'll take him up a cup of tea later. You have your breakfast then go out and do your chores.'

I blinked. We'd never had tea in bed before. 'Am I going to school today?' I asked.

'I don't think school will be on, what with all this snow. Wait till it melts, probably later in the week,' she said.

She passed me a plate with my two slices of bread and I munched them down, still scared about what mood Mr Gough might be in. He'd seemed completely mad the night before: mad and vicious.

'Morning, Terence,' he said in a normal voice when I appeared at the door of the cowshed. 'Where's your brother?'

'He's still asleep,' I said. 'He's not well. Mrs Gough is going up to him.'

He nodded. 'I've got the cows in, so you go and feed the horses and chickens, there's a good lad.'

I was glad he'd got the cows because it would have been difficult for me to manage without Dennis. It needed one person on either side to guide them the right way or they could suddenly run off towards the woods or the vegetable garden and give you no end of trouble trying to get them back.

Once I'd finished the animals, Mr Gough asked me to go and look for some firewood and I think there must have been panic written all over my face when I thought about what had happened to Dennis the day before when he hadn't found any.

'Just go up to the woods and see what you can find,' he said. 'If it's a bit damp, we can lay it out in the shed to dry off. Big strong lad like you can manage that, can't you?'

All his fury of the night before had dissipated and he was being reasonable, friendly even. I didn't dare look at him, scared of putting a foot wrong, because I'd so often witnessed the way his mood could turn on a sixpence. One minute he could be joking with us and the next he'd be screaming at the top of his lungs and handing out stripes.

I found an armful of firewood and laid it out to dry, and I cleaned the cowshed; then I decided to go back in and see if Dennis was awake. Mrs Gough was bustling round the kitchen, in a funny mood I couldn't make out.

'Is Denny up yet?' I asked.

'No, not yet,' she said. 'I took up his breakfast about eleven but he wasn't feeling very well so I said to him to stay there a bit longer.' She was wringing her hands. 'Could you go and shout Mr Gough for me? Tell him I need a word.'

I went and relayed the message to Mr Gough and followed him indoors.

'There you are,' Mrs Gough said to him as he took his boots off. 'Will you go up and have a look at Dennis for me? He's had another of his fits.' She glanced at me. 'Maybe we need to get the doctor to come out, if he can make it through the snow.'

Please let them get the doctor, I thought. Please, God. Maybe he'd be able to give Dennis something to help the pain.

Mr Gough was upstairs for a while and I listened hard at the stairs but I couldn't hear any voices. When he came back down, his face was set in a curious expression. 'He's in a pretty bad state,' he said to her, then he turned to me, where I stood by the door watching. 'Get back to your chores, Terence. We're dealing with this.'

'I've finished my chores,' I said.

'Go and clear the snow from the yard. Take the shovel,' he ordered.

I turned to go outside then hesitated. 'Can't I go up and see Denny? Just quickly?'

'No, not now. Maybe after the doctor's been. Out you go.' His tone was gruff but not unkind. As I said, you never knew where you were with him.

About half an hour later, I saw Mrs Gough running off down the path and I hoped she was going to phone the doctor. They had to use the phone at our neighbour Mrs Hillage's house because they didn't have one at Bank Farm.

It was a while before Mrs Gough reappeared and I ran across to meet her on the path.

'Is the doctor coming?' I asked.

She seemed very agitated, almost panic-stricken. 'He's out on call and I tried another doctor and he's out as well. Mrs Hillage is going to keep trying.' Suddenly she grabbed my chin and looked straight into my eyes. 'You have to tell the doctor that you and Dennis had been fighting. Will you remember to do that?'

'We hadn't been fighting,' I said, puzzled.

'On Friday last, in the yard you were. Remember? And we heard you fighting in bed last night.' She was gripping my chin hard, her nails digging in as she stared down at me.

'We weren't fighting in bed,' I said.

'Yes, you were. You were thumping Dennis. He's got red marks on his chest from it. And a couple of days ago you were fighting in the yard,' she insisted. 'Don't forget to tell them that.'

I didn't know who she meant by 'them'. The school?

'Is it lunchtime yet?' I asked.

'Yes, it must be, just about. Where's Mr Gough?'

'I think he's inside,' I said.

'Come and have your lunch.'

Mr Gough was sitting at the kitchen table with his head in his hands. He looked up as we walked in and Mrs Gough just said one word: 'Later.' He nodded. She served us all some lunch and I was astonished when she absent-mindedly poured me a bowl of the vegetable soup they were both having. What was going on? Would I get a row for drinking it, once she noticed?

I took a spoonful, and it was watery and a bit greasy but to me it was the most delicious food I'd ever tasted in my entire life. I gulped it down and wiped the bowl clean with one of my slices of bread so as not to miss one single drop.

Nobody spoke, and after lunch I was sent back outside to continue my work in the yard. I was there when I saw Mrs Gough rushing back down the path again, her coat flying open, her boots skidding on the snow that was starting to freeze over as the light faded. I took my time shovelling that part of the yard because it was a good position from which to see what was going on, and I was there when the doctor finally appeared wearing a big tweed overcoat and carrying a black bag.

Oh thank goodness, I thought. At long last Dennis was going to get help. He could give him something for the pain, and for his cough as well, and maybe he'd leave some cream for our chilblains. If he left some for Dennis, I could share it.

I went to the kitchen door, wanting to be on hand to hear what the doctor said, but when Mr Gough spotted me hanging around, he said 'Go and play outside, Terence. Don't you be getting under the doctor's feet.'

I was freezing cold by this time as the sun had gone down, despite the fact that it was still only mid-afternoon, so I sheltered inside the cowshed and peeked out the door. In my head I was thinking, hurry up, hurry up. I just wanted to see Dennis and tell him the amazing news that I'd had vegetable soup for lunch. Maybe they'd give him some as well.

When the doctor left, Mr Gough went running down the path after him and I heard raised voices but I couldn't make out what was being said. I ran to the kitchen door to ask Mrs Gough what the doctor had told her.

'He's had one of his turns,' she explained. 'I think he might have to go to hospital tomorrow.' She sniffed loudly, and I realized to my horror that she'd been crying. I knew she didn't care a jot about Dennis – she'd never been nice to him the way she sometimes was to me – so why was she crying because he was ill? None of it made sense.

'Can I go and see him now?' I asked.

'No!' she said quickly. 'The doctor said no one's to disturb him because he needs his sleep. You can sleep in your old room tonight, the one the Mullinder children were in.'

I was desperate to see Dennis but I didn't dare creep up without permission. Mrs Gough was there all evening, pacing up and down, and Mr Gough kept popping in and out busily. At teatime I had another surprise when Mrs Gough put a plate with two fried eggs and some fried bread in front of me.

'Get that down you, Terence,' she said. 'You need to keep your strength up so you don't get ill like Dennis.'

I couldn't believe my eyes but I didn't wait to be told a second time and I tucked into my tea with relish. Usually I felt a sense of dread right through teatime as I waited for the stripes I would be given afterwards but no one had said anything about a punishment that day. Would they suddenly remember something I'd done wrong? No. After we'd finished eating, Mrs Gough told me to go straight up to the Mullinder children's bedroom and get myself off to sleep. It was so early that I couldn't sleep straight away and I strained to hear their voices in the kitchen down below, but the doors and walls were too solid and all I could make out were murmurs. Why hadn't they let me see Dennis? I knew he would want to see me, no matter how poorly he was. We were all each other had. I considered waiting till the Goughs were asleep then creeping up to see him but the consequences if I was caught weren't worth thinking about. Besides, Dennis would be asleep himself most likely.

The next morning I got up bright and early and was out tending to the animals when I saw some men walking up the path. Three of them were wearing police helmets, and another two were carrying a stretcher, so I assumed they were the ambulancemen. I hurried down to the yard and watched as Mrs Gough let them in the kitchen door, but I didn't dare go inside in case I got told off for not doing my chores.

I went back to the chicken shed and started feeding the hens, keeping one eye on the door. About ten minutes later it opened and the two ambulancemen came out carrying the stretcher with Dennis on it. I couldn't see his face but I could make out a tuft of his dark hair above the sheet. The men were walking very carefully because there had been a fresh fall of snow in the night and the path was treacherous. I walked towards them, thinking that I could call out to Dennis to say 'Bye, see you soon.' I was a bit jealous of him going to hospital, remembering what a great time we'd had at St Woolos hospital in Newport, with the fantastic food and all the nice nurses.

A policeman stopped me before I reached the stretcher.

'Come inside, son. You must be freezing out here in just these shorts. Come and get warm.'

He put a hand on my shoulder and guided me inside, and I glanced one last time over my shoulder at the men who were carefully carrying my big brother down the path.

Inside the house, the Goughs were sitting at the table and the policemen were wandering all over the place, looking into every room as if they'd lost something.

'Where's Dennis gone?' I asked Mrs Gough.

'He's gone to a far better place than this,' she said without looking at me.

'Can I have his cigarette cards?' I asked.

'All right then,' she agreed. 'Dennis won't be wanting them any more.'

I thought she was wrong, that he would be asking for them just as soon as he felt better, but I decided to go and get them while I could. There was a policeman in our room when I got up there.

'Did you sleep in here as well?' he asked me. 'It's very cold, and it's awfully bare without any furniture.'

'It's OK,' I said, picking up the cards from the floor by the bedside.

'Look at your legs,' he said. 'They're all scratched to pieces. Come downstairs while I have a look at you.'

Clutching the cards, I went down to the kitchen and sat on a chair. The policeman tried to peel my socks off and I screamed in pain, because they were stuck to the burst blisters on my chilblains.

'Just look at the state of you,' he said, his voice all cracked and gentle. He turned to Mrs Gough and reproached her: 'Have you seen the cuts and sores on his legs? He's filthy as well. Look at this! Do you have any bandages in the house?'

She shook her head without looking at him.

'Get me a bowl of warm water then,' he said.

Normally I was scared of policemen but this one seemed very kind. He soaked my socks so carefully that they came away from my chilblains without pulling the tops off the scabs.

'These must be agony!' he exclaimed, and I agreed that they were, biting my lip to stop it trembling.

'Hang on a moment,' he said. He ran out of the house and was gone for a few minutes. I remained sitting on the chair and Mrs Gough kept herself busy at the kitchen sink, her back to me. When the policeman returned he had a first-aid kit in a tin. He smoothed some ointment onto my feet, then he dressed them with clean, soft, padded bandages. I had tears in my eyes because I wasn't used to anyone being so nice to me. I was also nervous about what Mrs Gough would say after the policemen left. Would I be in trouble for letting them see my chilblains? Would I get stripes tonight?

The other policemen came downstairs and one of them had a word with Mrs Gough but I couldn't hear what was said, except that at the end he said, 'We'll be in touch.'

Then he turned to me. 'Well, young Terence. Ever been for a ride in a police car?'

I shook my head, suddenly terrified. What were they going to do?

'It's all right,' the nice one said to me. 'You're coming with us. I'll carry you on my shoulders so your poor feet don't hurt.'

He put his hands under my arms and lifted me up onto his shoulders, so high that my head was nearly bumping the ceiling. We had to duck to get out the door, and it was then that I panicked and started screaming.

'No, don't let them take me away, Daddy!' I shouted to Mr Gough, where he stood watching from across the yard. I'd never called him 'daddy' before but all my fears about policemen came rushing back and I was sure they were arresting me and that I'd have to go to remand school. 'Where are we going? I don't want to go.'

'Calm down, Terry,' the nice policeman said. 'We're taking you somewhere nice, where you'll be looked after for a while. They can make your legs and feet get better. And I've got some sweets in the car for you.'

I stopped screaming then. That was good news. I hoped I would be taken to hospital and put in the bed next to Dennis's, as we'd been at St Woolos, and that we'd have beef stew and custard and the nurses would be lovely. It would be warm and cosy and no one there would give us stripes. I didn't have to be scared any more. A huge weight lifted off my shoulders. No one was going to thrash me that night. I wondered if we would get there in time for lunch? I was starving.

The policeman had to walk very carefully down the path with me balanced on his shoulders because the snow was several inches deep, even deeper in the hollows. As soon as we got in the car, he gave me some boiled sweets and I sat on the back seat, sucking them and peering out the window. Out on the main road, the snow was all melted and slushy. I could see snowmen in the front gardens of some houses, and I thought about the children who had made them, all wrapped up warmly and out having fun in the snow instead of having to shovel it up from a farmyard.

Our first stop was Shrewsbury police station. The kind policeman carried me in and sat me on the desk, but I was feeling scared again. All the events of the last two nights were running through my head and I thought I must have done something very bad to be brought to a police station, no matter what they said. Was it because Mrs Gough had told them about Dennis and me fighting or stealing food? Were they about to put handcuffs on me? I fingered the cigarette cards in my pocket and wished Dennis was there to tell me what to do.

I was taken into a nice warm room with two policemen and given a cup of sweet, milky tea and a plate of sandwiches, which I wolfed down. While I was eating they asked me lots of questions and scribbled down my answers. It was all a blur to me, but I answered as honestly as I could.

One of the first questions they asked was: 'Did you have enough to eat at the Goughs?'

'No, not really,' I replied, and immediately I felt nervous. What if they told the Goughs I'd said that?

'Did they ever hit you?'

'We got stripes when we were naughty,' I said, then showed them my roughened, calloused hands. The policemen seemed startled at the state they were in and I saw them exchange looks.

'What happened the night before last?' they asked. 'How did Dennis get hurt?'

So I told them about how he couldn't find firewood because of the snow, and that he took a bite out of a swede, and that Mr Gough had tied him to the pig bench and thrashed him, then he'd come upstairs and punched him while we lay in bed.

'Did you have a fight with Dennis that night?' they asked.

I said no, we hadn't. I wanted to ask where Dennis was and when I could see him but I felt too overwhelmed by everything that was going on so I just answered their questions without asking any of my own.

Soon we were back in the car again and driving through the streets of the town. It had got dark outside. Gas street lamps flickered, casting patches of orange light on the banks of snow that had been shovelled off the pavements. I wondered where I was being taken next? I was dying to see Dennis and talk to him about everything that had happened. They had to put us in the same place, didn't they? Surely they wouldn't separate us at a time like this?

We pulled up outside a big house, which the policeman told me was a children's home. He carried me inside and we were met in the hallway by a plump, pleasant-looking woman, who told us she was the superintendent, Mrs Bolton. We went in to her office and the policeman put me down in a chair.

'He can't walk because of his poorly feet,' he explained to her.

'It looks as though they're not all that's poorly,' she said. 'He has sores on his legs that could well be infectious, and he looks severely underweight. How are you feeling?' she asked me kindly.

I shrugged. I felt scared and I still felt hungry but I didn't feel as though I could tell either of them that.

She peered down at me, and her tongue made a clucking sound. 'I'm sorry,' she said to the policeman, 'but this boy needs medical attention. I suggest you take him to Shrewsbury General. He can come back here after they discharge him.'

My ears pricked up. That sounded like a hospital. I felt like punching the air in triumph when the policeman agreed he would take me there.

We got in the car once more and drove to the hospital, then I was put in a wheelchair and pushed up to a brightly lit ward, where the policeman said goodbye to me and the nurses took over my care.

'Is Denny here? My brother Dennis O'Neill?' I asked one of them, and she said she didn't know but promised to find out for me as soon as she could.

I was given a hot bath then tucked up in a warm, comfortable bed. The smell of the starched sheets took me right back to my stay in St Woolos hospital five years earlier, when I was only five. They brought my dinner on a tray – meat stew and mashed potatoes and carrots, then a sponge pudding – and I scoffed it in record time.

'You're starving, aren't you?' a nurse said to me. 'If you eat that fast, you'll make yourself sick.'

She was right; I did feel sick soon after, but I didn't mind because it was so nice to have a full stomach.

'Did you find out if Denny is here?' I asked before I drifted off to sleep.

'We'll see in the morning,' the nurse said, and stroked my head really gently. 'Someone will find out for you then.'

It had been a long day, a long couple of days, and I couldn't keep my eyes open. The bed was so soft and comfortable that my whole body relaxed and I sank into a deep, leaden sleep.

I was wakened the next morning by an orderly bringing round a tray of breakfast, and once again I ate it all so quickly that the kindly young man went off to make me some extra slices of toast with melting butter.

After breakfast, the curtains were pulled round my bed and a doctor in a white coat came to examine me, listening to my chest, looking in my ears, frowning at my sores and chilblains and chapped knees. He said I was severely undernourished and that I would have to take some vitamins and cod liver oil. He instructed the nurses on how to bandage my feet and what kind of ointment to use on my skin and then he swept out theatrically, the curtains billowing out behind him.

As at St Woolos, the nurses were lovely. They spoiled me with extra food between meals, and during their breaks they would sit and play card games with me, but when I asked about Dennis they all shook their heads and told me they hadn't heard anything yet. I supposed he must have gone to a different hospital, but I wished they would hurry up and find out.

Within a few days of arriving, I was allowed to get out of bed and walk around the ward, so I started doing little jobs to help out. I found I'd been put on an adult male ward rather than a children's one, and one of my jobs was taking urine bottles to the men who couldn't get themselves to the toilet for whatever reason, then to carry the full ones back to the nurses' station for emptying. I felt very important being allowed to help like this.

Four or five days after I arrived in the hospital, I took a urine bottle to a man whose bed was near the window. He gave me a funny look as I handed it over, then pointed out the window.

'Your brother's over there,' he said.

I turned to look and saw he was pointing at a churchyard across the square.

149

'No, he's not,' I said indignantly. 'He's in hospital. I saw him being carried off on a stretcher. I just don't know which hospital he's in yet.'

'He's not in any hospital,' the man said. 'He's beyond help now. Look at this.' He picked up the newspaper he'd been reading, the *Daily Mirror*. 'Your brother's dead.'

I just glanced at the paper without seeing it. There was a rushing sound in my ears. 'No, he's not!' I shouted at the top of my voice. 'You bloody liar!'

I ran back to my bed screaming so hard that my throat hurt and leapt under the covers. How could he say that? How could he be so cruel? He didn't know what he was he talking about. Two nurses came rushing over.

'Terry, shoosh. Calm down. Stop making such a noise. What's happened?'

Huge sobs erupted from my chest, making it difficult to speak. 'He said …' I sobbed, pointing at the man. 'He said Denny is … dead!' I couldn't get any more words out, too overwhelmed with emotion. I was desperate for them to tell me straight away that it wasn't true, that it was all a mistake, but they just looked at each other as if they were embarrassed. Why didn't they tell me he was lying? What did they know that I didn't?

At that moment, I realized. So it *was* true. Oh my God!

One nurse put her arms round me to comfort me and I sobbed hysterically, tears and snot soaking the shoulder of her uniform.

Later, I was taken to a consulting room and an older woman – I think she was the matron – tried to explain to me that Dennis had been very weak from his chest infection and his heart had just stopped beating. I listened hard, trying to piece it all together. They said he had already been dead when they carried him out of the Goughs' house on a stretcher. He hadn't been taken to hospital; instead his body had gone to a mortuary.

So when exactly had he died? Had he been alone at the time? Was Mrs Gough with him? The questions filled my head but I couldn't bear to put them into words. If the Goughs had got a doctor to come earlier that morning, would he have been able to save Dennis? Was there anything more I could have done during that last night when he was clawing my back in pain?

And then I thought about his white face and cold skin that last morning and an awful possibility occurred to me. Had he died in the night lying beside me? When I couldn't waken him, was he already dead? Had Mrs Gough been lying when she claimed to have talked to him after I got up?

And above all, there was one huge question: how on earth would I manage in the world without him?

I didn't ask the questions, though. I just shrank inside myself and stopped talking to anyone. The nurses were even more lovely than before, bringing me sweets and lots of extra food, stopping to hug me or stroke my head whenever they passed. I didn't want them, though. I only wanted my big brother. I couldn't get my head around the fact that I would never see him again. None of it seemed real. There was a pain deep inside me that felt as if I had been stabbed with a knife right through the heart.

Chapter Eleven

Over the next few days, I mostly stayed in bed with the covers pulled right up, clutching Dennis's cigarette cards, the only thing I had left of him. The nurses brought me food and I ate it, they came to dress my sores and I let them but without talking at all, and when they asked if I wanted a game of cards, I just shook my head. Occasionally I asked someone a question that came into · my head.

'Where is Dennis's body?' I asked one nurse, and she told me it had been taken to the mortuary in Shrewsbury. 'Can I see it?' I asked, but she told me that the police needed to do something called a 'post mortem' and I wouldn't be able to see it because of that.

'What's a post mortem?' I asked, and they told me it was tests so they could find out exactly what he had died of. They said there was always a post mortem unless people died in hospital of an illness the doctors already knew they had. It was so they could try to stop people dying of the same thing in future.

I thought about death the whole time. In particular, I thought about the lodger at the Connops' who was there one minute, marching round the village with a big smile on his face, and then he got sick and died and he was just gone. Life carried on without him. His room was converted back into part of the hall as if he had never existed. Is that what would happen with Dennis? Would everyone just forget him?

I wondered if Freddie had been told? Or our other brothers and sisters? What about Mam and Dad? None of them had known Dennis as well as I had. They probably wouldn't be that bothered, I decided.

And I wondered about God. Would Dennis be with him in Heaven already? How did that work? Would he definitely get in through the pearly gates after the naughty things he'd done, like stealing that swede from the Goughs' pantry? I couldn't think of anything else he'd ever done wrong in his life. I was the naughty one of the two of us. Surely God would look after him? I wondered if I should pray, but despite the best efforts of the Sisters of Charity school I'd attended at the Connops', I didn't know how to do it all on my own. I was too self-conscious to get down on my bended knees by my hospital bed, so I just pulled the covers over my head, pushed my hands together into prayer position and whispered in my head:

'Please, God, look after my big brother Denny.' And then I would usually start crying because I missed him so badly and what I really wanted was for God to send him back to me again.

One morning when I woke up I couldn't even remember Dennis's face. I couldn't picture it. I could see bits of him – his unruly black hair, his deep-set, sad eyes, and his hands with the black engrained under his nails and all the callouses and hard skin – but I couldn't get the bits to add up into a whole picture, and that made me cry a lot. I wished I had a photo of him. It felt disloyal not to be able to see his face in my mind's eye any more.

A couple of the other patients came over to try and comfort me but I refused to talk to anyone, and I stayed well away from the man who had told me Dennis was dead. I knew it wasn't his fault, but I didn't like the abrupt way he had said it, pointing out of the window at the churchyard like that.

A few days later, the doctor came round and examined me again and announced that I was well enough to leave, and my spirits plummeted to rock bottom because I assumed I would be taken back to the Goughs'. I couldn't face going back to that place and sleeping alone in the freezing cold room where I used to sleep with Dennis. I couldn't face Mr Gough's temper and the stripes every night. I knew there was no way I'd cope with conditions there without Dennis beside me, keeping me strong.

'Will the Goughs come and pick me up?' I asked the next nurse who came by.

'Oh, gosh, no!' she exclaimed, seeming flustered. She looked over her shoulder as if she wanted someone else to come and help her. 'You won't be going back there. I think you're going to a children's home for now. It's called Bellevue. You'll like it. I've heard very good things about it.'

'I don't want to go,' I told her. 'I want to stay here.' The tears came again and I brushed them away angrily. It's just that they had all been so kind to me in that ward, and I didn't want the disruption of moving and having to get used to yet another new place.

The nurse stroked my head really gently, and it felt nice. 'I promise it will be fine,' she said. 'I know it will.'

It was late one afternoon when a social worker came to take me from the hospital to Bellevue Reception Centre. He explained that I would only be there for a few days until a more permanent place could be found for me and I felt upset about this, but somehow I didn't have the energy to argue. I had no energy at all. I walked to the car and sat huddled in the back, and when we got to our destination I walked inside the building but I didn't manage to talk, or look around me, or even think about much at all. I just wanted to keep myself to myself, my thoughts locked away inside.

I was introduced to the superintendent of the centre and a couple of staff members and they all seemed very nice but I forgot their names as soon as I'd been told them. I was led into a dining room where I ate my tea on my own and then taken up to a bedroom where I was to sleep. Someone came in and painted the ointment on my skin, because it needed to be done for another week or so until the infection had completely vanished. She was a nice lady. She tucked me into bed and told me to try to sleep and not to worry about things because they would look after me and make sure I was all right now.

After she left, sleep was a long time coming. It was a small, very dark room, much quieter than the hospital, where I had dozed off listening to the nurses chatting at the nurses' station, and the older men rustling their newspapers or snoring. I missed those noises. I'd never been to a new place without Dennis before and it was quite intimidating. What if there were some bullies I needed to stand up to? What if the staff hit you here, as they had done back at Stow Hill? I'd always been brave in new situations before, but I only had the courage to be brave knowing that Dennis was right beside me. I didn't think I could do it on my own.

I must have dropped off to sleep at last, but I woke suddenly, screaming with terror, after a nightmare. For a few minutes, I didn't know where I was or what was happening to me. The nice lady who had put me to bed came rushing into the room and switched the light on. She was wearing a long nightdress and had curlers in her hair.

'It's all right,' she said, sitting on the bed and putting her arm around me. 'Don't be upset.'

I could only remember fragments of the dream. 'There was a monster roaring,' I said, shakily. 'It was coming towards me but I couldn't see it.'

'Oh goodness, I know what that was,' she told me. 'The main railway line from Shrewsbury is right outside. You probably heard a train going past. They can be quite noisy, especially on this side of the house. Do you want me to take you round to see the trains tomorrow?'

I nodded and lay back on my pillows, exhausted. Some time later I heard another train and it made the window-panes rattle as it passed. And then I went back to sleep again.

The next day, as she had promised, the woman took me for a walk round the corner so that I could see there was an overhead railway bridge running right alongside the house. Cars drove underneath a big stone archway while trains puffed by up above. It was a sunny day and all the snow had melted, although it was still bitterly cold and I could see my breath. They'd found me a coat to wear – a buttoned-up brown wool coat – and some new shoes, and even a knitted woollen hat, so I was cosy and warm in all that.

Suddenly I wondered what the Goughs were doing at that moment. How would they manage to look after all the animals without us? Maybe Bob Smith would have to come and help them more often, I decided.

I was starting to feel angry with the Goughs, whenever I thought about them. If only they had got the doctor back before Christmas when that woman from Newport Council asked them to, maybe Dennis would still be alive. If only they hadn't made him go into the water trough naked when he already had a bad chest. That couldn't have helped. Mrs Connop had always told us to stay indoors and keep warm when we had a cold or a cough, but they sent him out into the ice and snow. I blinked my tears away and tried to think about the trains instead.

Just as I'd been told, only a few days after I arrived at Bellevue I was being moved again, this time to Besford House boys' home, just up the road, the place where the policeman had taken me the first night I left the Goughs'. It was a large house in its own grounds, with a lawn at the front and a gravel driveway leading up to the front and side doors. It had playing areas at the sides and back of the house and, as I arrived, I saw lots of boys kicking a football around. I braced myself. I didn't feel ready to deal with a whole new group of boys yet. I knew I still couldn't talk to anyone about what had happened to me recently without the tears slipping out.

Which is exactly what happened when I was taken to meet Mr Bolton, the superintendent of Besford House. He was thin, with sharp features, in contrast to his plump wife, who I had met the night I'd been there with the policeman. We had a long talk the first day I arrived and he told me several things I hadn't known already.

'Do you know what an inquest is?' he asked, and I shook my head. 'Well, it's like an official court where a person called a coroner decides exactly what caused someone's death. He listens to stories from all the people who were there at the time, and from the doctors, and then he makes his decision. So the coroner is deciding about Dennis's death and he wants to talk to you.'

I was listening hard. 'What does he want to know?'

'He'll just ask you exactly what happened at the Goughs in the days before Dennis died, and you have to tell him the truth. He might ask about what you had for your meals, or whether Dennis had fallen over and hurt himself. I don't know the questions, but you'll be fine if you just say what you know. I'll come with you.'

'Will the Goughs be there?' I asked. There was a sick, nervous feeling in the pit of my stomach when I thought about seeing them.

'The coroner will want to talk to them as well, but not at the same time as you. We'll make sure you don't have to see them.'

That was a relief. I still worried that someone might decide I had to go back and live with them again and, after a couple of weeks of decent food and kind treatment, I couldn't face Bank Farm. I couldn't imagine how I'd ever put up with it for over six months. 'When do I have to talk to the coroner?'

'The inquest will be some time in February,' he said. 'I'll let you know. But in the meantime, I'm afraid you can't go to school because the coroner doesn't want you to talk to other people who might influence you. Do you know what that means?' I shook my head. 'Someone might say something that isn't true but it gets stuck in your head and you start thinking it must have happened. It's very important that you just tell the coroner the exact truth, so they want you to stay inside the home here until the inquest is over.'

That seemed fair enough. I didn't mind at all about not starting a new school straight away. There was a large playroom in the home where I could sit and read books, or play with the toys – they had a train set I especially liked. When the rest of the boys (there were about twenty of us) got home from school we went to play outside if the weather was good enough.

There was a grassy area about the size of a football pitch by the side of the house and they all seemed to like playing cricket there. It wasn't a game I'd played before but I watched for a while and picked up the basic rules then decided to join in. Someone handed me a bat and I went up to stand at the place where the other batsmen had stood. A boy bowled the ball towards me and, instead of hitting it with the bat, my footballing instincts took over and I stuck out my chest to stop it. I hadn't realized that cricket balls were rock hard and I was knocked over by the force of the blow, completely pole-axed and unable to catch my breath.

The other boys gathered around as I lay on the grass, panicking because I couldn't breathe. There was a horrible pain in my chest, and suddenly I thought I was having a heart attack and that I was going to die. There was a ringing in my ears and I couldn't hear what anyone was saying to me. Help me, Denny, I thought, as I gasped for breath, my heart beating like the clappers. Was this it? Was this what death felt like?

Someone had gone to fetch a member of staff called Joe, who came hurrying out onto the pitch. He helped me to my feet and led me indoors to sit down in the kitchen and have a cup of hot sweet tea. He kept talking to me, telling me I was fine, and gradually I realized I wasn't going to die after all. Not now, at any rate. When I told him how fast my heart had been going, Joe explained I'd had something called a panic attack. I felt shaky for ages afterwards. I just sat in the kitchen, watching as they got the tea ready, until I felt better. Next morning, there was a dark cricket-ball-sized bruise on my breastbone.

Joe was a youngish guy with dark hair, a sturdy frame and a big smile. I found out that all the boys liked him. Maybe it was because he was closer in age to us than the older staff members – he must have been about twenty-five – or maybe it was because he seemed to be on our side. He'd stick up for us if we wanted to go out to play when Mrs Bolton thought it was too cold, or if we asked for an extra snack in the evening. He seemed solid, like a father figure. Or a brother figure. Maybe he was my Dennis replacement during that period – I don't know.

All I knew was that I liked it when he was around. I felt better when I was with him. Before long, I would come down in the morning searching for his face, hoping he would be on duty that day because he was nice and he was fun to be around.

The dormitories were on the second floor at Besford House, and my bed was just beside the fire escape in the largest one. On the first Saturday I was there, we had to queue in the playroom for a dose of senna pods, a laxative that was given to all the boys fortnightly. It tasted absolutely vile, and we all made faces and shuddered as we swallowed our cupful, then we hung around waiting to see when it would start to work. Boys were rushing to the toilet, and standing in a queue hopping from foot to foot and grimacing as they tensed all their muscles to stop themselves having an accident.

The senna pods didn't work on me during the day, but I woke suddenly in the middle of the night and knew I needed to move my bowels urgently. So urgently, in fact, that I knew I would never make it down the length of the dorm and along the corridor to the toilet. There was no option. I opened the fire escape door and did my business on the metal steps outside, rather than soil my bed and have all the other boys make fun of me.

Next morning when the mess was discovered, the staff knew it was me – it had to be – but strangely, no one gave me a row. They were all being so nice. The cook kept slipping me treats, like a piece of buttered fruit cake or an apple, and no one ever told me off, even when I was being a complete pain.

I knew that other boys got sent to Mr Bolton to be caned if they were naughty, but it seemed I was to be spared any chastisement. One day I had a fight with another boy. He'd come over and started an argument and it came to blows. I completely saw red. I fought with all my strength, hitting, kicking and punching with all the pent-up rage that was inside me. I pushed him over and he bashed his head on a table, but still I kept hitting him when he was on the floor. I was completely out of control and Joe luckily pulled me off him or I don't know what would have happened.

I was in a terrible state afterwards, near-hysterical, and Joe sat with me, trying to calm me down. It was only later that I heard the other lad had to be taken to the infirmary for stitches to his head. I was sure I'd get caned for putting another boy in hospital. Every time one of the staff came into the playroom, I thought they were going to summon me to come to Mr Bolton's office and get my punishment.

But I wasn't. The fight was never mentioned again. The boy came back from hospital with neat black stitches on his forehead and he stayed out of my way from then on.

Chapter Twelve

On 13 February, a Tuesday, Mr Bolton drove me to Pontesbury Court for the inquest. It was only when he mentioned the date that I realized my tenth birthday had been and gone without me noticing and I told him as much.

He frowned. 'I thought your birthday was back in December,' he said.

'It was, but the Connops moved it to the third of February. That means I'm ten now. Ten days ago.' I felt I should have had some kind of celebration to mark the day, but there was no one to celebrate with. I hadn't received any birthday presents. Ten felt like a very grown-up age. When Dennis was ten, the Connops had made a huge fuss about it.

Despite Mr Bolton's assurances, I was still anxious that I might bump into the Goughs in the courtroom and I kept peeking round corners and glancing down corridors, but fortunately there was no sign of them.

I was taken into a room and introduced to a Mr Maddocks, an important-looking man in a black gown and woollen wig, who explained to me that when we were in court, he would be the first to ask me questions about life at the Goughs, and then the next day another man, called Mr Gough Thomas, would have some different questions. All I had to do was tell the truth.

I was overawed by the surroundings, the dark walls, people in smart suits rushing about, and the clerk of the court who kept shouting things that I couldn't understand, telling everyone what room to go to. Noises echoed in the stairwells and people rushed around in a hurry.

We were led into our courtroom and I saw four men sitting behind a long table, who all looked up as I came in. They seemed friendly, but spoke with posh accents that made me a bit ill at ease. It was very serious at the beginning, when I had to read out an oath from a card, swearing that I would tell the truth and the whole truth, so help me God. I caught Mr Bolton's eye and he smiled and gave me a thumbs-up. When I sat down, my feet didn't reach the floor because the chair was too big for me and I kept slipping down the seat.

The questions were easy enough that day. Mr Maddocks asked where Dennis and I slept at Bank Farm, so I described our bedroom and the covers we had on our bed. He asked about our meals, and I told him it was almost always bread and marg. Earlier on, we had occasionally been given a piece of trout, or some rabbit stew, but in that case we got fewer slices of bread. He asked what we had to drink, and I told him we had tea without sugar, and that we got milk at school.

Then he asked what happened if we were naughty, and I was struggling not to cry as I told him about the stripes. I said they were usually on our hands but sometimes on our legs, and that there could be as many as a hundred in one night if we had done a lot of bad things. 'What kind of bad things?' he asked, so I told him: 'Sometimes for going in the pantry, for taking a long time getting the horses in, sometimes for not cleaning out the cowshed properly and sometimes for getting our clothes dirty.' I couldn't remember any other reasons, although I knew there were lots more, but he seemed happy enough with that. I kept glancing at Mr Bolton and he was nodding at me, which made me feel more confident.

But when Mr Maddocks started asking about the last day of Denny's life, I couldn't stop myself bursting into tears as I described the way Mr Gough made him get into the water trough, then thrashed him on the pig bench, and how he came upstairs when we were in bed and punched Denny on the chest. In my mind's eye I could see his skinny naked body, shivering convulsively in the kitchen. He had wrapped his arms round himself and crossed his legs to try and protect his modesty, and he wouldn't look at me. He just kept shaking, his teeth chattering, and he was so

thin. Like a skeleton. Mr Maddocks passed me a handkerchief from his own pocket and I blew my nose loudly. I
couldn't bear to think back to that evening and the sheer
terror of it all.

On the way back to the home that afternoon, Mr Bolton
said, 'You did really well, Terence. I was very impressed
with the way you answered the questions so clearly. I think
the magistrate was impressed as well. Tomorrow is going
to be a little bit more difficult, though.' He paused. 'Mr
Gough Thomas might ask you more tricky questions, but
you just have to answer them as clearly and honestly as
you did today and it will be fine.'

I couldn't imagine what he meant. How could anything
be more tricky than answering questions about when you
last saw your brother alive?

I had a question for him, something I'd overheard
someone talking about outside the courtroom.

'Will Denny have a funeral?' I asked. I'd never been to
a funeral and had no idea what it was, but I knew it was
something you did in a church after a person died.

Mr Bolton paused for ages before he spoke. 'Your parents
already had a funeral for Dennis, down in Newport. I'm
sorry, but you weren't well enough to go. It was while you
were still very poorly, before you came to Besford House.'

'My parents?' I was astonished. 'Do you mean my real
Mam and Dad?'

'That's right.' He patted my knee. 'I'm sure they gave
Dennis a good send-off.'

I was surprised to hear they were even interested in Dennis after all this time without attempting to get in touch with us. Maybe mums and dads have to do your funeral if you die. Maybe there was a law about it. I wondered what had happened at the funeral – what did Mr Bolton mean by a 'send-off'? – but I didn't mind that I hadn't been there. I didn't want to see my parents. They didn't care about me, so I didn't care about them.

'Is Denny buried in a churchyard now?'

'Yes, in St Woolos churchyard in Newport.'

I shivered. That didn't appeal to me at all. I couldn't bear to think of Dennis's body under the ground, with all the earth on top of him. The thought made me feel sick and panicky.

'What's for tea tonight?' I asked, just to change the subject. There was only so much I could think about before my brain went all fuzzy.

The next day, the other counsel, Mr Gough Thomas, started out by asking me loads of questions about food. Did we ever have chicken at the Goughs? Or bacon, or eggs? Did we have syrup on our bread? Did we ever have meat? Or fishcakes? He was asking the questions so quickly that I got confused sometimes and said yes when I meant no, and a few times I just said that I wasn't sure. I couldn't remember.

Then he went on to a different subject: 'Did you used to fight with Dennis?' he asked.

'We used to quarrel a lot,' I replied tentatively, not sure if I should say this now he was dead. It seemed disrespectful.

'Do you remember one time when you got a stick and Dennis a spade and Mrs Gough came and took them off you?' he asked.

I was ashamed, so I said 'I don't remember', even though I did, but he pushed me and I had to admit I'd hit Dennis on the shoulder with the stick just a few days before he died. It made me very sad to remember that.

Then he started asking about whether we hit the calves and killed them. I admitted that I had hit one calf with a stick, but I said I knew I hadn't hit it very hard and I was sure that wasn't what had killed it. He asked about us kicking the chickens and I admitted it was possible that we could have kicked them, and then I burst into tears. This time the magistrate passed me his handkerchief and I held it to my face trying to calm myself down. I didn't understand why he was asking me all these questions. What did they have to do with Dennis dying?

Mr Thomas asked next about the beatings we got from Mr Gough. 'Were they the same as when you were given the stick at school?'

'No, they were harder beatings than at school,' I said. No one had ever beaten me as hard as Mr Gough had.

'Do you remember any days when you did not get the stick from Mr Gough?'

'Maybe one or two,' I said. When I was thinking about it afterwards, I remembered that he didn't use to beat us the previous summer when we first arrived at Bank Farm. It was only in the autumn when the days got darker.

'Do you want to go back to Mr and Mrs Gough?' he asked, and I replied 'No!' in as definite a voice as I could manage, and everyone in the court looked at each other.

I was kept in there for an hour and a half and when they dismissed me the magistrate thanked me for all my help and said I could go. On the way out, I saw the policeman who had bandaged my feet at the Goughs and he gave me a big smile.

'How are you doing, young Terence?'

I just had time to mumble that I was OK before the policeman was called in to the court and he gave me a cheery wave goodbye.

'Why is he here?' I asked Mr Bolton.

'He's going to tell the magistrate what he saw when he came to the farm that morning after Dennis had died.'

I nodded. That made sense. 'What happens now?' I asked once we were in the car on the way back to the home. 'Will the judge decide exactly what Denny died of? When will he tell us?'

Mr Bolton took a deep breath before he answered. 'They already know what Dennis died of. He died of heart failure, because his heart had been weakened by the lack of food and the beatings Mr Gough gave him.' He looked sideways at me. 'There's something you don't know yet, Terry, and I was asked not to tell you before the hearings this week, but Mr and Mrs Gough have been charged with manslaughter. That means that they will have to go on trial to find out whether their bad treatment of Dennis was the cause of his death, and if the judge decides it was, then they will go to jail.'

I was so stunned by this that I couldn't respond straight away. The word 'manslaughter' was horrible and didn't seem right somehow. First off, Dennis wasn't a man; he was only a boy of twelve years old. Secondly, slaughter was something you did to farm animals. Cows were slaughtered, not children. The Goughs hadn't slaughtered Dennis as far as I could see. They hadn't cut his throat with a knife, or wrung his neck the way they did to the chickens.

Mr Bolton continued: 'When grown-ups are put in charge of young children, they have a responsibility to look after them properly and that means giving them decent food and clothes and not letting them come to any harm.'

I could see that the Goughs hadn't done this. But would they be sent to jail for it? Both of them? What would happen to all the animals on the farm?

Mr Bolton carried on. 'What we just attended was a preliminary hearing where the judge will decide if the Goughs have to go on trial, and if they should be kept in jail until the trial or if they can get out on bail and go back to the farm. I'll let you know when that decision is made, because if they go to trial, you will be called as a witness again.' He caught the expression on my face. 'It will be just the same as you did today and yesterday. You'll have to answer all the questions as honestly as you can, and then people will decide if they are guilty or not guilty.'

Guilty. That was another word I pondered for ages. It would mean it was their fault Dennis had died. In my heart of hearts, that's what I believed now. They made him ill by not feeding him, and not giving him enough clothes so he was always freezing, and making him get in the water trough. They beat him. They didn't get him a doctor. I blamed them. I wanted them to go to jail.

But in that case, surely I was guilty as well? I could have told one of the teachers at school how ill Dennis was and asked them to get a doctor. I could have gone to the neighbour, Mrs Hillage, and asked her to phone someone. That night when Dennis was tied to the pig bench I could have stood up to Mr Gough and said 'Stop! You mustn't beat him any more.' Why hadn't I? I'd been too much of a coward, that's why.

Suddenly it was all too much and I burst into a fit of noisy hysterical crying. 'But … I'm guilty too,' I sobbed, choking out the words.

Mr Bolton braked suddenly, making me jerk forwards, and he pulled the car over to the side of the road. He took my face in his hands and turned it towards him so that I was forced to look him straight in the eyes.

'No, you are not,' he said firmly. 'Don't ever think that.'

'I could have gone for help!' I shouted, in floods of tears. 'I could have saved him!'

Still holding my face, Mr Bolton spoke slowly and very clearly. 'Do you have any idea how close you came to dying yourself?'

The shock of this stopped me crying and I stared at him wide-eyed.

'You were seriously malnourished, covered in infectious sores, with septic ulcers on your feet and bruises all over your body. If help hadn't come when it did, you wouldn't be alive yourself. One doctor said to me you were possibly only a week from death.'

My chest was heaving and a river of snot streamed from my nose. I just stared at him.

'There is nothing you could have done,' he continued emphatically. 'Nothing. You were too ill. You must always remember this. Is that clear?'

I nodded yes. He pinched my chin affectionately and started the car again and we drove back to the home.

Chapter Thirteen

After the preliminary hearing at Pontesbury, the Goughs were committed for trial and the newspapers were free to write about the story. Staff at Besford were very careful not to bring newspapers into the house because I wasn't allowed to see them, but I found out a bit about the newspaper coverage from the hundreds and hundreds of letters I began getting from members of the public – and, better still, presents.

The first day it happened, I was sitting on my own in the playroom after the other boys had gone to school. I looked out of the bay window and saw the postman driving up to the front door in his red van. He pulled out three large sacks of parcels and letters and I watched with curiosity as he carried them into the hall.

An hour or so later, Joe opened the door of the playroom and brought one of the sacks in. 'Guess who these are for?' he twinkled.

I looked at the address on the letter that was on top: 'Terence O'Neill, care of Besford House, Shrewsbury'.

'What are they?' I asked.

'Presents and cards from well-wishers,' he grinned. 'All for you!'

It was like every Christmas and birthday I had ever had rolled into one – and more. I decided to open the presents first: there were all kinds of Dinky toys – metal cars, trucks, fire engines, ambulances; there were Hornby electric trains; there were model aeroplanes, my favourite; there were huge boxes of sweets; there were teddy bears and books and board games and pencil cases with protractors and compasses and all sorts of pens and pencils. Soon the floor was strewn with wrapping paper and toys. All for me. I felt as though I was dreaming. Surely someone would realize there had been a mistake soon and come to take them all away from me again?

'Can I eat any of the sweets now?' I asked.

'Of course you can,' he said. 'Go ahead.'

I opened a box of toffees and popped one in my mouth, savouring the sweet, melting caramel taste on my tongue. As soon as the first one was reduced to sticky goo, I had another and then another.

When I'd finished unwrapping the parcels I turned to the letters. Some of them had money in them, and Joe said that Mr Bolton would put it into a bank account for me for when I was older.

The letters all said roughly the same thing: that I was a poor wee soul and that the Goughs were hideous monsters. Some of them offered for me to go and stay with them and said that if I were their little boy, they would buy me anything I wanted. Some of the offers sounded tempting but I decided that I wouldn't be able to tell from a letter whether they were good people or not. The Goughs had seemed OK at the beginning. I didn't want to take the risk of ending up in another bad situation.

When the other boys came back from school, they all wanted something and kept grabbing at presents I hadn't even opened yet. I felt this wasn't fair. The public had sent them to me because of what I had been through. I gathered all my new possessions into a pile in the corner and guarded it. 'Can't I just have one box of sweets?' 'You've got two racing cars – can't I play with one?' 'Just a toffee? Go on. You'll never manage them all yourself.' People kept pestering me and I was getting more and more upset. 'No, they're supposed to be for me,' I kept saying, close to tears. I was so sensitive in those days that tears were never far away.

Eventually most of the boys backed off. 'Just leave him on his own,' someone said. 'Greedy guts. Hope you get a stomach ache.'

They went to play outside but I didn't dare leave my new pile of possessions because a few kids were hanging around, still trying to change my mind. All evening I guarded my presents, unable even to play with the aero-planes freely in case someone sneaked a sweet while I wasn't looking.

Joe came to have a word with me. 'You might be popular with the public who are sending you all these presents, but you're not very popular with the boys you live with. Why can't you share your sweets at least? You've got enough to last you a year there.'

'I don't know if I'm supposed to,' I said. 'They were given to me.'

'There's plenty for everyone,' he reasoned, 'And you'll probably get more in the days to come. You can't possibly manage them all by yourself. What's more, if you share with the other boys, it will help you to make friends with them. You want friends, don't you?'

After he said I could, I handed out some sweets, and most of the boys were grateful, although some still made sarky comments about me being a miser.

When we went up for bed that night, I realized that people were still behaving oddly around me, despite the fact that I'd handed out my sweets. No one joked with me in the bathroom, and no one said goodnight when we climbed into bed. What had I done wrong now? They were just jealous, I told myself. Tough luck for them! But inside I felt very lonely and upset.

Over the next few days I realized that the mountains of presents I received weren't the only reason I was unpopular with the other boys in that home. It must have been galling for them that I got away with so much. The staff treated me like a prince and slipped me second helpings at meals, or turned a blind eye if I sneaked sweets up to the dorm at night, which was against the rules. I suppose I became a bit arrogant, thinking I could walk on water if I chose to, and I pushed it too far.

I was in the playroom one evening and I got into a bit of banter with another boy, teasing him and winding him up.

'Say that again and I'll hit you,' he threatened.

'You wouldn't dare,' I replied. I felt safe in the knowledge that a member of staff would step in and protect me if he got violent. Surely he knew that as well? 'Go on, I dare you, cowardy custard,' I taunted.

Suddenly he snapped and charged across the room and punched me in the stomach so hard that I lost my balance and fell. I looked around but there were no members of staff in sight.

I pulled myself up from the floor. 'I'm going to tell on you,' I said. 'You've had it now.'

I made my way out of the room and told the first staff member I could find, Mrs Bolton, who had always been especially nice to me in the past. 'Serves you right,' she said. 'You've been getting a bit cheeky lately.'

That threw me. I'd thought I was the favourite. Where was my special treatment?

It didn't take long before I realized that being singled out for special treatment meant that none of the boys wanted to be friends with me. I was teased about being

'Mr Bolton's pet'. I still hadn't been sent to his office for a caning, although some of the other boys were there every couple of days for one misdemeanour or another – many of them things I got away with. Who did I want to be friendly with? The staff or the boys? I decided I wanted to stop being called a 'pet' and I worked out a plan.

They hated bullying in that home and always came down on it like a ton of bricks. One evening, while there was a staff member present, I walked up to one of the littlest, youngest boys and hit him. I didn't punch hard – it was just for show – but he started crying all the same.

'Terence, what are you doing? Get straight up to Mr Bolton's office!' the staff member ordered.

I marched noisily up the stairs, making sure as many people as possible saw me.

'What did you do that for, Terence?' Mr Bolton asked sadly. 'Was he being horrible to you first?'

'No,' I shook my head. 'I just think he's an idiot.'

'You can't go through life hitting everyone you think is an idiot.'

I ramped up the bravado. 'He'd better keep out of my way or I'll hit him again,' I boasted.

Mr Bolton studied me closely as if he could see right through me and I wondered if he knew what I was doing and why. 'You must realize that I can't let this go unpunished,' he said. 'I hate to do this to you after your recent experiences, but you leave me no option. Stand up and hold out your hand.'

He gave me three strokes of his cane on the right hand and three on the left. They didn't really hurt – it was nothing compared to the stripes I'd received from Mr Gough – but as soon as I left his office I went to soak my hands in cold water to relieve the stinging. Then I went straight downstairs, walked up to the same poor boy and hit him again.

'What are you doing, Terence? What's got into you?' the staff member on duty cried. 'Go straight back up to Mr Bolton's office.'

I could tell Mr Bolton was getting annoyed this time, and he hit me a bit harder with the cane. Once again, I went straight downstairs afterwards and punched the unfortunate boy I'd chosen as my target that evening, who had done nothing to deserve it. Once again I was sent back up to Mr Bolton's office. This time he was really cross with me. He picked out a walking stick from the umbrella stand and hit me once on each hand with it. That really hurt, so I rushed off to soak my hands in cold water and I didn't repeat the offence.

My plan worked. After that, the other boys stopped calling me 'pet' – there was respect, no matter how reluctant – and gradually I made friends with a few of them. It was much more fun having someone else whizzing aeroplanes through the skies with me, because then we could have a proper Battle of Britain game, something I couldn't have done on my own.

On 26 February, almost two weeks after my last court appearance, it was time for the Goughs' trial to begin at the Shrewsbury Assizes, a criminal court overseen by high court judges. The day before, Mr Bolton sat me down and explained to me that there would be lots more people in the courtroom this time. He told me there would be twelve members of a jury, the counsels for the prosecution and defence, the judge himself, members of the public who were allowed in to watch from a gallery up above, and he explained that the Goughs might be there in court. He said they would be guarded by policemen so I had nothing to fear from them, but I couldn't get to sleep that night for worrying about seeing them face to face. It gave me the shivers to think of it.

When we got to the courtroom next morning, there was a long queue of people snaking out of the door and right down the road. They were mostly women, wrapped up against the cold in fur coats and hats, and all looking very smart. Mr Bolton led me straight in past them but I heard some voices in the crowd saying 'That's him! That's Terence!' before we pushed through the doors and an official led us into a waiting room.

We'd been told the hearing would start at ten-thirty and that both counsels would make opening speeches then I would be called, probably after lunch. Mr Bolton had a newspaper with him, and I'd brought a book, but in fact I just sat on the wooden bench, swinging my legs and feeling nervous. It had been hard enough answering the questions I was asked at the last court, but now I would have to do it with all those people present, and the

Goughs watching me. My chest felt tight and there was a big lump in my throat. What if they couldn't hear me? What if I couldn't get the words out?

I listened to the noises in the corridor outside – people chatting to each other, doors swinging, the clerk of the court shouting out instructions – and I wondered if the Goughs were there already. They must be. I hated the thought of even being in the same building as them. What if the door opened and they walked in?

It went quiet outside and I guessed they were all in the courtroom. Time passed and Mr Bolton kept glancing at his watch. 'They should break for lunch soon,' he said. 'I expect someone will come and tell us what's going on.'

Suddenly there was a rap on the glass panel in the door and Mr Bolton got up to see who was there. 'It's probably a newspaper photographer wanting to get a shot,' he said.

I walked over beside him and saw two people standing outside – an older man and woman – and realized they were shouting my name.

'Open up, Terry. We just want to say hello.'

I peered at them.

'It's us,' the woman shouted. 'Your mam and dad.'

Mr Bolton looked at me for confirmation, but I shrugged. I didn't recognize them at all.

'Open the door, Terry,' the man shouted, grinning at me.

I looked at Mr Bolton and he looked at me, then we opened the door and went out into the hallway.

The man stuck out his hand. 'How are you doing, son?' he asked.

I shook his hand and said 'Fine.' Then the woman grabbed me for a clumsy hug. 'My poor boy,' she kept saying. 'Poor baby.'

'Your brother Tom's here as well,' the man said. 'He's just round the front. We queued for hours but couldn't get into the courtroom so we thought we'd try and find you in here.'

I didn't say anything. Were these really my parents? Sure enough, the woman had a funny eye, as I know my mam had, but I didn't remember anything at all about the man. Still, the last time I'd seen my dad had been when I was four years old, so maybe that wasn't surprising.

'Are they treating you all right?' Mam asked. 'Are you OK now?'

'Yes, fine,' I said, too overcome by the moment to say any more. Afterwards, I thought of some questions I could have asked them – about Dennis's funeral, and about how my other brothers and my sisters were – but I didn't say anything at the time.

'We'd better get back in the waiting room now,' Mr Bolton said. 'If you want to see Terence, you can come to Besford House some time. Call to make an appointment first.'

'Bye, Terry,' Mam said, waving gaily.

'Bye son,' my dad said, then Mr Bolton closed the door and we sat down to wait again.

'That must have been a bit strange for you,' he commented, but I just shrugged and shook my head. It was no stranger than everything else in my life at the time. I'd felt no connection with those people but at least it had taken my mind off the waiting for a while.

Suddenly there were noises in the hall outside, doors opening and people talking. The volume rose. The door to the waiting room opened and the clerk of the court came in.

'I'm afraid you've had a wasted journey today,' he said. 'The trial has been postponed and it will be heard at Stafford Assizes now instead of here.'

'Why? What happened?' Mr Bolton asked.

'The defence counsel argued that Mr and Mrs Gough should have individual counsel rather than being represented by the same person, in case their stories contradict each other's. Also, the judge was worried that there might be prejudice if the trial was heard in this area, where people know so much about the case. He reckoned that there will be more chance of a fair trial in Stafford. You'll be informed about the revised court date. Meanwhile, you are free to go for today.'

I felt a huge weight lift off me at his words. I had a reprieve. But then I realized I would have to go through this whole experience again – arriving at yet another courtroom and sitting waiting with a knot of nerves in my stomach until I was called in to testify.

'Will the Goughs be allowed to go back to the farm now?' I asked, worried about what would be happening to the animals. I missed those horses, for all the trouble they used to give us sometimes.

'No, they're in jail,' Mr Bolton told me. 'They're selling the farm.'

That was good, I thought. Someone else could look after the horses, someone who would be kind to them and not hit them with a pitchfork.

In the car going back to Besford House I thought about all the strange things that had happened that day: the queues of women in fur coats waiting to see me; my mam and dad appearing; and then the case being postponed after I'd got myself so worked up into a lather about it. I felt all at sixes and sevens with the turmoil and my stomach was churning. I wished life could go back to normal. But I knew it couldn't. Not yet. There was still the trial to get through, whenever that might be.

Chapter Fourteen

The Goughs' trial at Stafford Assizes was set for 15 March 1945. Mr Bolton drove us there and as we walked into the court, I noticed lots of photographers with big cameras that flashed as I walked past. I wondered if my picture would be in the newspapers. I thought I'd like to see a copy if it was.

We went into the courtroom and this time the clerk led us to a corridor where he said to sit and wait till we were called. I sat, as before, swinging my legs and trying not to think about how nervous I felt.

'Will you wait there for a moment while I go to the gents'?' Mr Bolton asked me, and I nodded.

He'd only been gone for a short while when a door opened somewhere along the corridor and as I glanced down, my heart stopped beating. Coming towards me was the unmistakeable figure of Mr Gough, with his black hair and deep-set eyes, wearing a light-coloured Mackintosh instead of his usual rough farming clothes. He saw me at exactly the same moment that I saw him and our eyes met.

I let out a yell and leapt to my feet and sprinted off down a corridor in the opposite direction. I had no idea where I was going – I just wanted to get as far away from him as possible. I heard footsteps chasing after me and my name being shouted – 'Terence! Stop!' – so I ran even faster. Then I felt a hand on my shoulder and screamed as loudly as I could, struggling to get away, until I realized the voice wasn't Mr Gough's. I turned to see the clerk of the court. He was holding on to my coat to stop me running off.

'It's OK, he's gone. He's in the courtroom now. Calm down. He can't get you. You're safe here.'

I burst into tears, in a delayed reaction to the shock. 'I don't want to do this,' I sobbed. 'I don't want to be here.'

'Of course you don't. It's a terrible thing for a young boy to go through.' He patted me on the back. 'You've been so brave. Everyone says so.'

I let him lead me back to the corridor where we were supposed to wait. My knees were like jelly and I wondered who on earth had said I was brave? I didn't feel brave. I felt like a quivering wreck that morning. Tears were still slipping out and I wiped them with the back of my hand, hoping no one would notice.

The clerk explained to Mr Bolton what had happened and he put his arm round my shoulders and gave me an awkward pat. 'I'm so sorry, Terence. I shouldn't have left you on your own.'

We sat down again to wait, but now my tummy felt so stirred up that I was worried I was going to have to get to the toilet urgently. What if I needed to go while I was in the court? Even worse, what if I had an accident in there with everyone watching? I told Mr Bolton I had to use the toilet and he came with me, which I was glad about. What if Mr Gough had been in there? As soon as I got into a cubicle, my stomach clenched and I was sick into the toilet bowl.

'Are you all right?' Mr Bolton called, but when I tried to reply I was sick again, and I kept on throwing up until my stomach was completely empty.

I rinsed my face in cold water and washed my hands and felt a bit better. Mr Bolton straightened my hair for me with a comb.

'OK now?' he asked, and I nodded, but when I looked in the mirror my face was white and my eyes were all red.

When we went back outside, he told the clerk that I had been sick and next thing a doctor was called. He took my pulse and asked me whether I felt dizzy or if I thought I might be sick again. I told him I was fine, and at last they agreed I would still be allowed to testify.

Maybe it was a good thing I was so worried about my tummy because I had less time to worry about what I was actually going to say in court. When I was called in not long afterwards, I didn't look around me. I was vaguely aware of Mr Gough standing in a boxed-off area to the side. Mrs Gough was there as well, in a pale blue coat, and a woman in uniform stood between them. There was a gallery up above packed with people, and the judge at his big desk, wearing a wig and a black cloak, and then some other men in wigs and dark suits.

'Come and sit near me, Terence,' the judge said, indicating a chair. 'My name is Justice Wrottesley.' He explained to me how to say the oath, with my hand raised, and I didn't tell him I had done it before at Pontesbury. I just repeated the words as I was told then sat down. It was then I saw a pig bench in the corner of the courtroom and my tummy started clenching again. What was that doing there?

One of the men in wigs got up and started talking to me. I must have looked a bit off because he said 'It's me, Terence. Mr Maddocks. Remember?'

I nodded, although to be honest all those men in wigs and black gowns looked the same to me.

'Your Honour, I should tell the court first of all that Terence hasn't been very well this morning.'

'What seems to be the problem?' the judge asked me.

'I've been sick,' I said quietly.

'You must tell me if you feel unwell and we'll take a break,' the judge told me, and I felt glad about that. He seemed nice.

Mr Maddocks started asking me all the usual questions: about what we had to eat at Bank Farm, where we slept and about getting stripes from the Goughs.

I cried a little while I was talking, but it wasn't too difficult because I had answered all these questions before. I just looked at the judge and Mr Maddocks and pretended there was no one else in the room. I didn't look at the Goughs at all.

Then he started asking about the last day Dennis was alive, when he couldn't find firewood in the spinney and Mr Gough tied him to the pig bench and beat him.

'Could you show us how Dennis was tied to the pig bench?' he asked, and I had to get up and bend over the wretched thing, demonstrating how Dennis was tied onto it cross-wards. It felt horrible. I was conscious of all the people in the court looking at me in the little grey suit that Mr Bolton had given me, and I felt shy and nauseated and scared all at the same time.

While I was describing the night of 8 January, when Mr Gough came upstairs to punch Dennis on the chest as he lay in bed, the judge asked me to demonstrate how he had punched him so I stood up, put my knee on my chair and mimed him punching with all his strength.

'Did you ever thump Dennis in the night?' Mr Maddocks asked.

'No. I pushed him out of my way in bed but I never thumped him.'

'Did Mrs Gough tell you what you were to say to the doctor when he came?'

'She told me to say I thumped him.'

Suddenly there was a cry: 'This is all lies!' and with a shiver I recognized Mrs Gough's voice.

'The defendant will be quiet in court,' the judge said sternly, then turned to smile at me. 'You're doing very well,' he told me. 'Carry on.'

After Mr Maddocks had finished his questions, a man called Mr Bourke stood up and the judge explained to me that he was defending Mr Gough. He started by claiming that the Goughs had paid us for working on the farm, which confused me. He said Mrs Gough had given us tuppence for cleaning the chicken shed and we put it in our money boxes.

'You used to get some money every week, didn't you?' he asked, and I said I didn't remember that. I had no idea what he was talking about but I told him we got money for selling blackberries at the village shop.

He asked about the food we had been given, then he interrupted and told me that my story was different now than what I'd said at Pontesbury because there I'd said we got milk at the farm and I'd just told Mr Maddocks we didn't. I felt as though he was calling me a liar. He went through all the types of food that we were supposed to have had, and I was desperately trying to remember what I'd said at Pontesbury, but in truth if we had been given cheese or salmon or rabbit, then it happened so seldom that I couldn't think of it. Maybe it had happened back in the summer when things were all right, but I had no memory of it.

Mr Bourke asked a lot of questions about the fight I had with Dennis in the yard, when I had a stick and he had a shovel. He made me stand up and demonstrate for the court exactly how I had hit him. He told the judge that Mrs Gough had to catch Dennis as he nearly fell over after I hit him, and that later she heard Dennis threatening to kill me.

I shook my head, puzzled by that. What was he talking about?

He said that we used to fight a lot and that once Bob Smith had to break up a fight between us. I said I didn't remember that. I was beginning to feel very upset by the questioning. It sounded as though he thought that I had been the one who killed Dennis rather than the Goughs.

Then Mr Bourke said that when Dennis and I walked into the chicken shed we used to kick the chickens.

The judge turned to me and asked, 'Did you kick them for fun or because they crowded round you?'

I started crying at that point. It felt as though everyone was ganging up on me and accusing me of things I hadn't done, and I couldn't find the words to explain the truth. I hadn't realized it would be like that.

'I think we should adjourn for lunch,' the judge announced, and I was led out of the courtroom and back to where Mr Bolton was waiting for me in the corridor.

'Why are they saying all those things about me?' I sobbed. 'I'm not lying. I'm telling the truth.'

'I know you are,' he soothed. 'You're doing fine. The thing is, the Goughs are trying to lie their way out of trouble by blaming you, but no one believes them. Everyone believes you. The judge is on your side, so don't you worry about him. You're not the one on trial here.'

We sat and ate some sandwiches they had made for us at Besford House, and they helped to settle my stomach a bit. At two o'clock, the clerk came to call me back in again.

'Just be strong and tell the truth,' Mr Bolton urged me.

Straight away, Mr Bourke was back on about those chickens but I tried to be more definite in my answers this time.

'Did you sometimes kick the fowl?' he asked.

'I only shooed them,' I replied.

'Did you and Dennis beat the calves?'

'We just smacked them when they would not go up from the field.'

At last he stopped going on about the animals that had died and started asking about our Christmas presents, and about Mr Gough trying to play mock-boxing with us, and he tried to make me admit the Goughs had sometimes been nice to us.

'When you and Dennis were good boys, Mr and Mrs Gough were kind to you, weren't they?'

'Once, I should think that would have been.'

'And when you were good they gave you extras, didn't they?'

'I don't think they did.'

I got the feeling he wasn't very happy with my answers, but I was only telling the truth.

After Mr Bourke had finished his questions, another man in a wig stood up, this one called Mr Long. The judge told me that he was defending Mrs Gough. I could see straight away what he was trying to do because he asked me if I could remember times when Mrs Gough tried to make Dennis sit down and have some food, but Mr Gough had sworn at her. I said I didn't remember that. He asked if I remembered a time when she tried to stop Dennis going outside in wet socks and Mr Gough over-ruled her. I didn't remember that either.

In response to his questions, I said that I did remember the Goughs arguing with each other. I agreed that the morning when Mrs Gough threw her clogs at Dennis, they hadn't actually hit him. There were various other details like that, where Mr Long tried to make out that Mrs Gough had been on our side and had tried her best to protect us from Mr Gough's temper, but I didn't agree with that. She could have given us food while Mr Gough was out working. I remembered her sitting with a blank expression the night Dennis was thrashed on the pig bench. She could have intervened, could have tried to help him, but she didn't. She had never liked Dennis much, I don't think.

Mr Long's questions finished and the judge thanked me and told me I could go. 'You've been very helpful,' he said. 'We may have to ask you to come back again, but we'll let you know about that.'

I walked out of the courtroom with my head down so I didn't have to look at anyone. I still hadn't looked directly at the Goughs. Mr Bolton was waiting outside.

'Well done!' he said. 'Everyone could tell you were speaking the truth, especially the judge and the jury. You've got nothing to worry about, Terence.'

I became quite angry later that day when I thought about how the Goughs had been trying to push the blame on to me. I suppose that's why they had brought up the stories about the chickens and the calf dying – so that everyone would think I was rough and cruel. They might think that if I was capable of killing animals then maybe I killed Dennis. But I just didn't believe that the taps I gave those animals could have killed them. They were nothing compared to the cruelty I'd seen from Mr Gough, especially that day when he attacked the horses with the pitchfork. Maybe I should have told the judge about that.

I had a chat with Joe that evening about my worries, and he said 'Judges are very wise men, Terry. They can see through lies and they understand human nature. He won't believe for a second that you could have killed those animals. Just look at the size of you! You're a pipsqueak!'

I felt better after that but I went to bed soon after tea, tired out from the day's events. Mr Bolton said I'd been on the witness stand for three hours altogether, which is a long time to be answering questions. Also, I didn't want the other boys asking me what had happened. I didn't feel up to talking about it.

I was called back to the court one more day that week, just very quickly, to clarify some answers I had given about the food. It seemed that the Goughs weren't registered with a butcher, despite them claiming that they fed Dennis and me plenty of meat. I confirmed that I barely remembered having any meat at all while I was there. They also asked about a night when Mrs Gough kissed me and Mr Gough got cross. I couldn't remember the night they were talking about but I did say that Mrs Gough told me not to kiss her when he was around – which was fine, because I never tried to kiss her anyway. It was only her kissing me, and I wasn't that keen on it.

As we left the court that day, a woman in the crowd outside shouted 'Murderer!' at me. I turned around, stunned. She was a stout woman with a round red face and she was shaking her fist at me.

'Keep walking!' Mr Bolton instructed. 'Don't stop.'

When we got to the car, he explained: 'It's because the newspapers reported the Goughs' defence this morning, and some very stupid people will believe it. But only until the jury comes to their verdict. Then everyone will know the truth.'

Still, my ears rang with the word all the way back to Besford House. There was a horrible taste in my mouth, like metal. How could she say that? How could she think I would kill my own brother?

'Don't give it any more thought, Terence,' Mr Bolton told me. 'She was obviously mad.'

At the end of the week, he called me up to his office to say that the jury had delivered their verdict. Mr Gough had been found guilty of manslaughter and Mrs Gough was guilty of wilful neglect. I nodded. I'd thought this would make me happy, but it didn't help particularly. It didn't bring Dennis back, did it?

'I want to tell you what the judge said to the jury about you.' He read out from his newspaper: '"You should trust your own observations. You have seen Terence, heard him cross-examined, and you can tell he has nothing to hide. Of course he was often naughty, as I expect you were when you were his age."' Mr Bolton looked up and smiled at me. '"In cross-examination that little fellow was quite ready to admit some things which had not been part of his original story, and with regard to others he said 'No, that did not happen'. His evidence is corroborated" – that means it ties up with what the doctors found and what other people said. So they believed you, Terence. I knew they would.'

'What will happen to the Goughs now?' I asked. 'How long will they be in jail?'

It was the following Monday when we heard the sentences. Mr Gough had got six years and Mrs Gough six months. Mr Bolton told me the judge's comments to them. He said to Mr Gough: 'You have shown beastly cruelty and your behaviour has, I think rightly, shocked the world and shocked England.' To Mrs Gough he said: 'Your upbringing told you what your duty was, and you did not do it. Nobody can but agree with what the jury has said.'

I hoped the stout woman who shouted 'murderer!' at me would read those remarks. I hoped she would feel sorry for what she had said.

I thought about the Goughs sitting in their prison cells, and I imagined them wearing striped pyjamas, like a picture in a story book I had seen, with bread and water rations, and a tiny barred window giving the only daylight. It seemed fair to me that they should be in jail. I was glad.

A couple of weeks later, Mr Bolton told me there was going to be a government inquiry to find out why Dennis and I had been placed in the care of a couple who hadn't been checked out by the authorities, and to work out how they could stop the same thing happening to any other children in future.

'Will I have to go and answer questions again?' I asked.

He said he didn't think so. I'd said all I could in court.

After that, I decided I'd had enough of it all. I wanted to get back to being a normal boy again. I wanted to go to school and play with my friends and not be known as the one whose brother had died any more. I wanted to be the same as everyone else.

I took all my memories of Bank Farm and most of my memories of Dennis and I put them in a box somewhere right at the back of my mind and I pretended it hadn't happened. It was easier that way. If I didn't think about Dennis, I didn't have to walk around with that big weight of sadness on my shoulders and the tears always pricking behind my eyes.

At night, I quite often woke the dormitory with my shouts as I emerged from a terrifying dream I couldn't quite remember. But by day, I was Terry O'Neill, the mischievous lively lad again.

Chapter Fifteen

After the trial was over, at the end of March 1945, I was allowed to start attending Town Walls Catholic School in Shrewsbury. It was a big school built on the side of a steep hill overlooking the River Severn, and it took about half an hour to walk there from Besford House. We'd go in groups: across the river on a steel footbridge called Greyfriars Bridge, then up a steep hill to the town centre and along to the school. I liked watching the boats on the river: long working barges with boxes of cargo, and pleasure craft such as rowing boats, sailing boats and the like. There were usually swans dodging around them, followed by their cygnets which used to squawk anxiously if their mothers got too far ahead.

The school was on such a steep slope that the tarmac playground was useless for ball games; the ball would just have rolled away down towards the river. On games days, we had to march up to the top of the hill, past the Catholic church, to the playing fields which were on level ground.

Every Friday we attended Mass up at that church. The girls were all supposed to wear hats and if they had forgotten to bring one, the nuns would give them one from a props basket belonging to the school's drama department. Some of them were very odd creations to see on a young girl's head: battered granny-style straw hats or a velvet beret with pheasant feathers sticking out the side that had been used for a production of *Robin Hood*. There would be so much giggling in the aisles at these ridiculous hats that very little attention was paid to the service.

I settled in reasonably well at the school and made a few friends. But I had a scare one afternoon as I was waiting outside school for a couple of boys to walk into town with me. A man was standing leaning against a wall on the other side of the road and he called out to me: 'Come here, little boy.'

I glanced over my shoulder but there was no one else around so he had to be addressing me. He repeated it, so I went over to see what he wanted.

'Would you like some sweets?' he asked.

I stepped a bit closer and suddenly he grabbed my wrist, put his arm round me and lifted me up on top of the wall. It was about my height on the pavement side, but on the other side there was a sheer drop down towards the river.

'What are you doing?' I cried. He had a funny look in his eye and I suddenly felt scared. I jumped off the wall in a panic, hurting my feet on the pavement as I landed, then I sprinted all the way back through the town, across the bridge to Besford House. It didn't occur to me to tell a teacher in the school because I didn't know them very well. I ran straight up to Mr Bolton's office and managed to gasp out the story, despite being completely out of breath and having a stitch in my side.

'Let's go and find this man,' Mr Bolton said straight away. 'It sounds as though he might be a bit funny in the head and we should tell the police about him.'

We got into the car and drove up to the school but I couldn't see the man anywhere. When Mr Bolton asked me what he had looked like, I just said that he was old, with short hair, and wearing a raincoat of some kind. It wasn't enough of a description to go to the police with, so after touring the streets for a while, we drove back again.

'Don't let it worry you,' Mr Bolton told me. 'You did the right thing. If anyone offers you sweets like that, you should always run and tell an adult.'

'What did he want from me?' I asked.

'Who knows? Maybe he just wanted to chat, but you can't be too careful.'

I felt quite shaken up about the incident, but it didn't stop me going into town afterwards. I was wary of any strangers who tried to talk to me, but I enjoyed wandering around and looking in the shop windows too much to be put off by one peculiar man.

Some of the boys at the home collected stamps and stuck them in albums, and I was keen to try it. We were given pocket money every week and I used mine to buy an album, some paper hinges and my first set of stamps. There was a shop in town called Miss Pye's Antique Shop, which sold wonderful stamps of all shapes and sizes with fantastic colours and pictures. I quickly learned to recognize which country a stamp came from, and I liked the exotic ones with palm trees, or the Chinese or Japanese ones with funny writing, or the different-shaped ones, like the triangular ones from the Cape of Good Hope.

I'd sit at a big table with the other boys who liked stamp collecting and we'd spend hours planning the layout of our albums. I liked to colour-coordinate my pages and make patterns with the different shapes of stamps. We would trade our duplicates, and the deals were negotiated keenly. There was great rivalry over who got the best of a swap, and there were certain stamps we all wanted to get our hands on. One boy had a Penny Black, the first stamp ever used. Another boy only collected stamps with animals on them. We all wanted to get the ones with printing errors, like the American 'Inverted Jenny', because they were so valuable – but I don't think any of us ever did.

One or two of the boys were still mean to me, calling me names, or 'accidentally' knocking my stamps onto the floor as they passed. I still got occasional parcels with presents from members of the public so it may have been that they were jealous. Mr Bolton asked an older boy called Bill to look out for me, acting as a kind of 'minder', and that helped a lot. He was a really nice lad. If any of the bullies looked threatening, Bill just told them to leave off and that usually worked.

We often listened to the radio in the evenings, and followed the news as the enemy surrendered across Europe: first of all the Italians surrendered to American forces at the end of April, then we heard that Hitler had shot himself, and then the Germans finally surrendered on 7 May. The next day we didn't have to go to school because there were celebrations in the streets. Flags and banners were hung in the streets, a military band played, there was a march-past of the Armed Services and the Air Force, and then we all jumped out of our skins as they fired a big gun salute. The grown-ups were all hugging each other and laughing. We were waving our own little British flags on sticks and running around, weaving in and out of the crowd and cheering every time someone shouted 'Hip, hip … hooray!' It was an amazing feeling. We'd won! I think all of us boys took it personally, as though it was *our* victory. I felt exuberant, and very proud to be British that day.

A couple of weeks after this, one Saturday, I'd been delivering some 'letters' for Mr Bolton. In fact, I found out from Bill that they were betting slips. I often did this for him on Saturdays and he used to pay me a shilling.

On the way back I popped into the stamp shop to spend my earnings. I was browsing happily through the different packs, trying to decide what to buy, when the shop door opened and in walked a man. Out of the corner of my eye I could see he was medium height with dark hair. I turned to look at him properly and let out a yell of terror. It was Mr Gough!

Panic-struck, I hurtled past him out of the shop and sprinted all the way down the street, still yelling. Why was he out of jail so soon? I thought he was supposed to be kept in for six years. Had he come looking for me to get revenge for all the things I said about him in court? What was he going to do to me? I didn't stop running all the way back to the home, petrified that he was right behind me. I burst into Mr Bolton's office without knocking.

'Mr Gough is in town. He's out of jail! I saw him!'

'Terence, sit down, calm down,' he told me, putting his pen down on the desk.

'It's true. He came into the stamp shop!' I realized my hands were shaking. I think my whole body was probably trembling.

'It can't be true,' Mr Bolton said firmly. 'He's definitely still in jail. I think I know what's happened. Mr Gough has a brother who lives near here. I saw him in court a couple of times and they looked quite like each other. I expect it was him you saw.'

I took a deep breath. Could that be the case? I'd been so sure it was him. Maybe it was his brother though. I considered that. 'Won't his brother be angry with me for what I said in court? Will he try to get revenge?'

'Definitely not,' Mr Bolton told me. 'I expect he was horrified at what his brother did, just like everyone else in that courtroom. There are some things you can't forgive, even within a family. Put it out of your head.'

I did my best to forget it but after that, whenever I went into the town centre for the next few months, I tried to make sure some of the other boys came with me and I peered carefully down each street to see if there were any dark male figures coming our way.

No matter how hard I tried to keep the experiences at Bank Farm locked away in the back of my mind, I kept getting reminders from one direction or another.

On a Saturday morning towards the end of May, just a couple of months after the trial, a boy accused me of knocking a glass of water all over his stamp album. It wasn't me. I'd come into the room and seen the water all over the table but it had happened before I arrived. This boy was convinced I was the culprit and went to tell the member of staff on duty.

'Terence, I want you to apologize straight away,' she said. 'That's an awful thing to do.'

'But it wasn't me, miss!'

'Don't lie. You're only making things worse.'

I refused to apologize and she kept insisting that I had to. 'You won't get any breakfast until you apologize,' she said. 'Stand behind your chair.'

My face burned scarlet. I stood behind my chair, and instantly I was back in the Goughs' kitchen watching poor old Denny standing with his hands behind his back looking on sadly as I ate my bread and marg and the Goughs tucked into their food. I couldn't think of anything else but the sheer awfulness of that time: the crackling of the fire, the dusty room, the cooking smells, the Goughs chomping on their meal, and poor Denny standing silently waiting for the stripes that would be administered after we'd eaten. My chest felt tight with tension.

'Are you ready to apologize yet?' the woman carer asked me. 'You'll stand behind your chair during every single meal until you do.'

But I wouldn't apologize for something I hadn't done. My stubborn streak took over and I stood behind my chair through lunch as well without saying a word. I did wonder if she had any idea that we had been forced to do this at the Goughs'. Did she know what I'd been through? I didn't say anything, though.

That evening at teatime, I was once again standing behind my chair while the others ate their food, when Mr Bolton came into the room.

'Why aren't you sitting down?' he asked me.

The member of staff explained that I was being punished for not apologizing.

'Sit down, Terence,' he said straight away. 'Eat your food.' He took that staff member outside the dining room for a 'chat', and I don't know exactly what was said but she looked mortified when she came back in.

'I'm so sorry,' she mumbled to me. 'I didn't know.'

Joe was the one person in the home I could talk to. He always listened to anything I had to say and made time to sit down and have a chat, while most of the others just did their job of making sure we were washed and fed but didn't really get to know us. Joe and I would have a laugh and a joke and I felt I was special to him.

No matter how hard I tried to pretend otherwise, my emotions were still all over the place. I couldn't have put into words what I was feeling because I swung from being scared and panicky to being wild and naughty, or just a bit noisy and over-excited. I always felt I had to watch my back, as though I wasn't completely safe.

One day I was playing up a bit just as Joe came on duty. He came upstairs to the dormitories and I called out 'Hi, Joe!' but he walked straight past, completely ignoring me.

'He doesn't like you any more because you've been naughty,' a boy told me.

I felt a terrible pain in my heart and I ran downstairs to the dining room where I found a quiet corner and cried my eyes out. I couldn't bear the rejection from someone I had considered my safety net, the one person I could trust. I sobbed so hard I could hardly breathe any more. Who could I turn to if Joe wasn't my friend any more? What would I do? Without Dennis, and now without Joe,

I felt utterly alone in the world. The only people who cared about me were gone.

When Joe found me later, I was still in a terrible state, with swollen red eyes, shuddering with emotion.

'What on earth is wrong with you?' he asked, coming straight over to put an arm round me.

'It's because you weren't speaking to me earlier,' I stuttered, still feeling overcome.

'What do you mean? When wasn't I speaking to you?'

'On the stairs. You walked straight past me when I said hello.'

He looked surprised. 'I'm sorry, Terry. I just didn't see you. My mind must have been elsewhere.'

I wiped at my tears with the sleeve of my shirt. 'So are we still friends?' I asked in a timid voice.

'We'll always be friends,' Joe told me. 'Always.'

I felt foolish then for getting so upset. Joe helped me up and we went outside to join the others in a ball game, but I was shaky for the rest of the morning. I didn't like crying like that. It always left me feeling drained and fragile, as though I might break.

Soon after that, it was the summer holidays and the boys like me who had no families to go to were sent to a seaside holiday camp at Rhyl in North Wales. We stayed in big wooden huts near the beach, grouped round a play area with swings and seesaws. As soon as I arrived, I ran straight down to the sand and kicked off my shoes to paddle in the chilly water. I felt shy being in a new place with lots of strangers and I decided I'd spend as much time as I could on my own, just walking on the beach and exploring.

The staff at the camp gave me a woollen swimming costume to wear, and a towel. We were warned that there were strong undercurrents on the beach and not to go out too far but it was a hot summer's day and I was keen to get in the water. I still couldn't swim but it was nice to cool down. Imagine my embarrassment when I came out to find that the swimsuit that had fitted me perfectly before had now become heavy with water and sagged down to my knees! At the age of ten, I was old enough to feel self-conscious about my body and I tried to grip the sides of the costume and hold it up until I could grab my towel and wrap it round me. I wasn't so keen on the water after that.

One day I ventured out to the swings and was surprised to see the little Mullinder children on a seesaw. I suppose all the kids in our area who didn't have families to go to were sent to the same camp. They came running over to me to say hello, and the boy told me they were fine, that they were staying in a nice home near Shrewsbury. I told them they were very lucky that they hadn't stayed at the Goughs, because they weren't good people.

'I know,' the boy said. 'We didn't like him. He hit my sister on her bottom.'

If only that were all he had done, I thought, but I didn't say any more. They were too young to be told what a lucky escape they'd had.

Some days our group went for cross-country walks through the woods and fields nearby. We were supposed to follow a narrow footpath so that we didn't get lost and fall into any of the deep crevices scattered around that landscape but one day a few of us disobeyed orders and went off to explore the rest of the woods. We had a great afternoon, climbing trees and collecting hazelnuts, which we stuffed into our pockets. We got a huge telling-off from the camp attendants once we were back, but I enjoyed the freedom of the day. I was getting a taste for walking, especially on my own. Once we returned to Shrewsbury, I started going out for long walks round the town. I'd cross the river on the English Bridge then walk along and come back over the Welsh Bridge, watching the river traffic and thinking my own thoughts.

I was still getting letters and gifts from members of the public from time to time and that autumn, I had a visit from a soldier. He was Scottish, from the Orkney Isles, and he said he'd been very moved by my courage when he read my story in the papers so he decided to get in touch. He was a kind man, who told me lots of stories about his wartime experiences in the deserts of Egypt and Sudan, and he also described to me the remote island where he had grown up, and where he had to catch a ferryboat to get to school in the morning. He was still in the army, stationed at a camp near Shrewsbury, and whenever he was on weekend leave he came to take me out for afternoon tea and buy me presents. I don't know where his money came from but he spent a lot on me. My favourite present was for my eleventh birthday that December when he bought me a cut-out theatre that I treasured. It was my favourite possession for a long time and I played with it whenever I had free time.

Just after Christmas the soldier went back to the Orkney Isles and he phoned me at Besford House on 9 January, the first anniversary of Dennis's death, which was a difficult day for me. It was nice of the soldier to ring but it was a very crackly line and I could hardly hear him, which was sad because it was the last time I ever spoke to him. A few weeks later, I was told that a new foster family had been found for me, down south in Cardiff, and that I would be moving there on 4 February.

I can't remember the Scottish soldier's name now but I will always remember his kindness to a very mixed-up, sad little boy. There was nothing in it for him. He just wanted to spend time with me and help me to realize that there are good people in the world as well as bad. He and Joe, and Mr Bolton of course, are the three people who got me through that first year after Dennis died. As far as I know my own parents never attempted to get in touch again after that brief meeting at the courtroom.

It had been a funny old year all in all. A lot of the time I didn't recognize myself because I kept behaving in ways

I'd never done before. I felt lonely and vulnerable and scared without Dennis to protect me, but instead of letting anyone see that vulnerability, I covered it up with cockiness. Sometimes the emotions refused to be suppressed any more and they burst out in a big mess of tears and shouting and defiance. I yearned to be close to the other boys but my behaviour tended to drive them away, so I spent a lot of time on my own. I felt as though I was living inside my own head, and it wasn't a very nice place to be. There was a wall between me and the rest of the human race. I was different from them, marked by what I had been through. Life would never be the same again.

Chapter Sixteen

I was nervous about going to new foster parents. For a start, how did I know for sure they wouldn't turn out to be like the Goughs? Mr Bolton reassured me that they had been thoroughly vetted by social services, and that there would be regular visits to make sure I was happy there. He told me that the government inquiry after my court case, led by someone called Sir Walter Monckton, had made a long list of recommendations regarding the way in which foster parents were chosen, and the number of supervision visits that must be carried out once children were in foster homes.

'Thanks to you,' he told me, 'no other children will have to experience what you and Dennis went through.'

I felt quite proud of that. At least Dennis wasn't being forgotten if all these important people were still talking about him. But it didn't bring him back, of course.

On the morning of 4 February, the staff fussed around me, combing my hair and getting me dressed in my grey suit, the one I'd worn to testify in court, and all that made me even more nervous. It was as if there was a whole flock of butterflies in my tummy, all fluttering around. The hardest thing was saying goodbye to Joe. He said I could come and visit him any time, but I think I knew in my eleven-year-old head that that wasn't very likely and in all probability I'd never see him again. I held on to him for ages when we hugged but I managed to hold back my tears because lots of the boys were watching and I didn't want to seem like a cissy. I was suddenly very popular with them because I'd said I would leave behind all the toys the public had sent me, pretty sure I'd get more with my new family.

A lady from Newport Council came to pick me up and we got the train from Shrewsbury down to Cardiff, a journey I spent glued to the window. I couldn't stop thinking about the train journey I'd made with Dennis on the way to the Goughs, but I didn't tell her that. I kept quiet and looked at the world flashing past outside. When we arrived in Cardiff, we had to catch a tram to Canton, the district where my new foster parents lived. It was the first tram I'd ever seen and it looked like a strange bus on metal wheels that ran along grooves in the road, with a pole connecting it to the electric cables above. When we got to a crossroads, the driver would stop the tram while the conductor used a long, hooked pole to adjust the electric connections up above so that we took the right route. We were on the tram for about twenty minutes and although the wooden slatted seats were uncomfortable, I found the vehicle so fascinating that I forgot to be anxious about where I was going.

The nerves came back full strength when we jumped down from the tram and started walking along a street of terraced houses with bay windows and small front gardens.

'Number two,' the woman from the council said. 'Here it is.' She walked up the path and rang the doorbell then there was a long pause. No one came. It was only when she used the knocker that we heard footsteps inside; then the door opened and a pretty woman with light brown curly hair was standing smiling out at us.

'I'm so sorry. Have you been there long? That bell doesn't work,' she said. 'Come on in. You must be Terence.' She gave me a friendly smile and my first impression was that she looked OK.

I had a cup of tea and some digestive biscuits in the kitchen while Mrs Torjussen chatted to the social worker in the front room. Then the social worker left and I was on my own with a complete stranger who was to be my new foster mother.

She started chatting to me, telling me about the family I'd be living with. 'We're Norwegian originally,' she said. 'That's where the name comes from. There's my husband and three boys, all much older than you. Ronald is thirty,

Peter is twenty-six and Herman is eighteen. You're only eleven, aren't you?'

I nodded.

'The boys will look out for you. We all want you to be happy here. I know you've been through a terrible time but this will be a fresh start for you.'

Her husband and sons came back at teatime and I could tell straight away they were a nice family because there was lots of laughing and teasing and banter. The atmosphere was very relaxed, and I was delighted when fish and chips were served for our meal. Mr Torjussen made a joke when I dropped a chip on the floor – 'What did that one do to offend you?' – instead of telling me off. I liked my bedroom as well: it had a huge bed with the softest pillow I'd ever come across, and a comfy mattress and plenty of covers. It was like the Connops' – but maybe even better than that, because I got to eat with the family, as if I was one of them. That night I didn't have any nightmares but slept straight through. Next morning, when Mrs Torjussen served bacon and eggs for breakfast, I knew for sure I was going to be happy living with them because I'd had two of my all-time favourite meals when I'd been there less than twenty-four hours!

'Why don't you call us Mum and Dad?' Mrs Torjussen suggested. 'We'd like that.'

'I don't mind,' I said, but when it came to it the words didn't sound right in my head or feel right in my mouth. They weren't my mum and dad; I hardly knew them, so it felt odd to call them that. For the next couple of days I tried to avoid calling them anything at all. When I was sent out to the garage to tell Mr Torjussen that dinner was ready, I just told him, 'She said to tell you dinner's ready.'

They soon realized I was having trouble saying the words, so Mrs Torjussen suggested that I called them auntie and uncle instead, and that felt a lot more natural.

It was a Friday when I arrived, and on the Monday I was enrolled at St Mary's School, a primary school run by nuns, the fourth school I had attended in as many years. It was always intimidating when I was led into a new classroom; all those pairs of eyes looked up to assess me, and I wondered which one was the class bully and which were the friendly types. It was often humiliating when I found I was way behind in the work because I'd missed so much schooling with all my moving around. I hated it when the teacher asked me a question I couldn't answer and I could hear the rest of the class sniggering because they all knew it. But in fact, I settled in quite quickly in St Mary's and made a few friends: a nice boy called Terry Parle, who let me play in his den in the woods, and took me home for meals with his family, and some naughtier boys, with whom I got into a few scrapes later on.

In the Torjussen's back garden there was an air-raid shelter full of rusty old junk. When I crept inside, it smelled of damp, mingled with rust and mildew. There was a workbench crammed full of rusting tools, and shelves covered in different-sized screws and bolts, but the thing that caught my eye straight away was a decrepit old bike. Both tyres were flat and the brakes were hanging off but I was dying for a bike of my own. I saw other boys at school zooming around on theirs and I would have done anything to get one.

'Why don't you take it to the cycle repair shop down the road?' Mrs Torjussen suggested. 'See if it can be fixed.'

When the man in the shop saw the state it was in, he frowned, but I think he wanted to be nice because I was new to the area. Perhaps he knew who I was and what I had been through. After examining it, he said, 'It'll cost you two shillings and sixpence for me to fix that up. That suit you?'

'Yes, please,' I said quickly.

I raced home to tell Mrs Torjussen the news and she agreed that she would give me the money.

At the end of the afternoon, I went back to the shop with the money in my hand and the shop owner wheeled out my bike. It had new tyres, new brake levers and brake blocks, and it was all shiny and clean as well. I jumped in the air and shouted 'Yes!' when I saw it, and the shop owner grinned at my obvious delight.

No one had ever taught me how to ride a bike so I just got on and wobbled down the road, putting my feet on the ground to help me keep my balance if need be. A few weeks later, I decided to try a proper outing to Barry Island, which was about seven miles away. There was a fun fair there, with roundabouts, a big wheel and a roller-coaster called the Big Dipper. I had brought my pocket money along with me but I was too nervous to go on the Big Dipper because everyone riding it was screaming at the top of their lungs. I bought an ice cream and a bottle of pop and just wandered round looking at all the amazing things I had never seen before: sticks of pink rock with the name 'Barry Island' printed right through the middle; fluffy candy floss like pink clouds on sticks; jangling fruit machines; and shooting galleries where you had to try and knock a coconut off a pedestal. The noise and the colours and the flashing lights were spectacular, a whole new world I'd had no idea of before.

On the way home later, there was a steep hill. I started going down carefully but the wheels were turning faster and faster, the bike got out of control, and when I came to a sharp left-hand bend at the bottom, I knew I wasn't going to make it. I let go of the handlebars and dived sideways onto a grass verge, where I lay winded for a moment or two. When I sat up, the bike was lying on its side and didn't seem to be damaged but there was a rip in the knee of my trousers – the Sunday best trousers that Mrs Torjussen had only just bought for me. My heart sank. I remembered her saying specifically that morning that I was to take care of my new clothes. What would she do? Would I be beaten for this? Would I get no tea tonight?

While I was sitting on the grass verge worrying, I spotted some wild flowers growing in the hedgerow, so I decided to pick a big bunch as a peace offering. When I arrived home and opened the door, I held them out first, before she could see my trousers.

'They're lovely! Thank you so much, Terry,' she exclaimed.

I watched as she put them in a glass jar on the kitchen windowsill, then when she turned back towards me, I admitted 'I had an accident on my bike,' and stuck out my knee to show her.

'Oh no!' she said in a disappointed voice and made a little tutting sound. 'Are you all right, though? You're not hurt? That's the main thing.'

She managed to mend those trousers so the rip hardly showed, and after that her son Herman took me out for cycling lessons so I could learn how to ride my bike properly. He ran behind me holding onto the saddle while I practised and before long I was a lot safer on the roads.

I had another new experience not long after I arrived at the Torjussens: going to the pictures. There were three cinemas not far away in Queens Street and my school friends and I were obsessed with films, often going to as many as two a week. I loved all the Tarzan movies and Westerns, especially ones with Gene Autry or Roy Rogers and his horse Trigger. I loved *Last of the Mohicans*, and was also keen on *Great Expectations*, which came out in 1946.

My pocket money didn't stretch to quite so many cinema outings, but I had various devious ways of getting in. Sometimes I asked people passing by if they could spare a penny so I could catch the bus home, and when I had collected enough I would join the queue for the film I wanted to see. If it was an A certificate film, meaning children should be accompanied by an adult, I would give my money to a grown-up in the queue and ask them to buy my ticket for me and most were happy to oblige. Once I asked two old ladies, who not only paid part of the ticket price for me, but who also bought me a bag of sweets.

One cinema was easy to sneak into: we just walked in through the back door to the men's toilet, then out the other side of the toilet into the darkened cinema. We'd root around on the floor for used ticket stubs in case the usherette asked to see our tickets and we always got away with it.

Mrs Torjussen was very generous and as well as giving me pocket money she usually bought me whatever I asked for, but I decided I wanted to earn my own money. First I got a paper round that paid ten shillings a week, but after I got soaked in torrential rain one morning, Mrs Torjussen persuaded me that it wasn't worth it. Next I worked as a grocery delivery boy, riding a big heavy bike with a large carrier on front and taking people's groceries to their front doors. I enjoyed that work. I also used to make some money when Cardiff City Football Club was playing at home. Supporters parked their cars in the side streets near us and I would offer to look after them for a shilling apiece while they were at the match. I'd even wash their car for them for two-and-six. I could manage to look after up to twelve cars at a time, which was a good afternoon's work. Yet another money-making scheme of mine involved collecting old clothes from neighbours and selling them to the rag-and-bone man. He only gave me a few coppers though, and once he paid me with a goldfish in a plastic bag – which wasn't much use for getting into the cinema!

One group of lads I used to hang around with was prone to getting up to mischief, and one day they introduced me to shoplifting. We were standing in the toy department of a big store in St Mary Street when one of the boys said 'Contact' in a low voice.

I looked at him, wondering what he meant.

'Contact,' he said again, urgently, and suddenly the whole group of boys took to their heels and ran out of the shop. I hurried after them and, when I caught up, I found that they had all stolen something from the shelves. They explained that 'contact' was a code word meaning that the coast was clear. When anyone said 'contact' it meant we had to pick up whatever was in front of us and leg it.

I wanted to be accepted as part of the crowd, so next time we were in a shop and someone said 'contact' I stole a toy deep-sea diver and raced outside, where I gave it to one of the other boys. I didn't want stolen goods myself. I had all the toys I needed. Besides, I knew the Torjussens would be disappointed in me. And I thought about how my brother Tom had gone to an approved school for stealing pop bottles. I certainly didn't want that to happen to me.

Mrs Torjussen never found out what we got up to, but I knew she didn't like me seeing that crowd of friends and was always trying to persuade me to go out with Terry Parle instead. She signed me up for his scout troop and we went to scout camps together and took part in lots of fund-raising ventures for them, such as collecting glass jam jars in a big bogey cart then selling them back to the jam factory. She also approved when I became friendly with the man who owned the bike repair shop and started helping him on his allotment at weekends.

Life was busy and I didn't have too much time for brooding about Dennis but there were still moments when I yearned to talk to him. One day a boy told me to meet him for a fight behind the cinema after school. I'd been in fights before but never one that was planned in advance like this, and I was incredibly nervous as I made my way there. What would Denny have told me to do? I didn't want to fight this boy because I wanted to be his friend, but I felt I had no choice. In the end, I just went for it, the fight was over quite quickly and no lasting harm was done. But it reminded me yet again how much I missed my big brother looking out for me.

I wondered what Dennis would say about the shop-lifting. I got a feeling he would have told me not to be such an eejit. I wished he could have come to the cinema with me, because I know he would have loved cowboy movies and it's sad he never got to see a single film in his life. Most of all I wished he could have been with me at the Torjussens, where the food was great. They couldn't have been more generous towards me.

I didn't ever think about my other brothers and sisters, or consider the fact that they probably still lived just a few miles away in Newport. They hadn't been part of my life for such a long time that they hardly ever entered my thoughts.

One Sunday afternoon, Mrs Torjussen called me down from my bedroom to say that there was a brass band playing down the street, a Salvation Army band, and did I want to go and hear it? I had never heard a brass band before so I headed out and followed the sound of the music until I found them. They were playing 'Onward Christian Soldiers', accompanied by loud drumbeats and cymbal clashes, and it made me remember all the school instruments I'd stolen from the Sisters of Charity when I stayed at the Connops'.

Suddenly I realized that a young man playing the trumpet kept staring at me. I looked back, wondering if I knew him from somewhere. When the hymn finished, he put down his trumpet and came across to speak to me.

'Excuse me, is your name Terry O'Neill?'

'Ye-es,' I said slowly.

'I thought so! I'm your brother Tom.'

I looked at him closely and saw that it must be true. Something about his eyes reminded me of Dennis. I hadn't seen Tom since I was four years old, before I was taken away from Bolt Street, but he looked a bit like me, albeit seven years older. He would have been nineteen by this stage and was of medium height and stocky, with fairish hair worn in a short-back-and-sides style. He was wearing Salvation Army uniform. I gazed at him for a few minutes, unsure what to say, then I was suddenly overcome by confusion. What did he expect of me? What should I do?

I turned and ran back up the road to the Torjussens' house and burst in the front door.

'Auntie, it's my brother Tom! He's outside!'

'Don't be silly,' she said. 'None of your family knows where you live.'

Just then there was a knock at the door. Tom had followed me up the road.

'Hello there,' he said. 'I'm Tom O'Neill, Terry's brother.'

'Goodness me!' Mrs Torjussen exclaimed. 'What a small world it is. You'd better come in for a cup of tea.'

Tom came in to the kitchen and sat chatting for a while. He said he was in the Salvation Army, stationed just outside Cardiff, and that he was still in touch with the rest of the family back home in Newport.

'Did you hear about Dad?' he asked, and I shook my head. 'He died last year. Heart problems. He was never right after all that time he was stuck in the water at Dunkirk.'

When I had seen him at Stafford Assizes two years earlier, he had seemed perfectly fine. I tried to find the right expression to react to the news. 'That's a shame.'

'Yeah, he was still a young man, really. Only fifty-four.'

Fifty-four sounded old to me. I didn't care about Dad dying because I'd never known him, and I stopped listening to what Tom was saying. I just kept watching his face, because lots of little expressions reminded me of Dennis. I wasn't sure how I felt about seeing him. None of the family had come to see me in the home after Dennis died. They hadn't sent Christmas or birthday presents, or even just a letter saying how sorry they were for what I had gone through at the Goughs'. It seemed to me that all my problems had started with them, and I didn't want them back in my life now.

Before long, Tom stood up. 'I'd better get back to the band. They're a trumpet short without me! But I'll come and see you soon and maybe we can go out for a day together. How would that be?' He grinned and patted me on the shoulder.

A couple of weeks later, good as his word, Tom turned up along with my brother Charlie.

'How're you doing, kid?' Charlie asked. 'Fancy going to the pictures with your two big brothers?'

I can't remember what film they took me to. I just remember walking along the road and feeling dwarfed by them, one on either side. I got the impression that Mrs Torjussen didn't entirely approve of me going out with them but didn't feel she could say no. It might have been because they were a bit rougher-looking than her family and the neighbours round about. Maybe she thought they weren't a good influence. Or maybe she just worried that it would be unsettling for me to see them.

I wasn't bothered one way or another whether I saw them or not. It felt too late to develop a proper brothers' relationship like I'd had with Dennis. You needed to have the same life experiences for that, and we'd gone in completely different directions.

Not long after I was back in touch with Tom and Charlie, a journalist turned up on the doorstep one day with a photographer in tow. I could hear from the living room as Mrs Torjussen talked to them on the doorstep.

'We wondered if Terry would be willing to tell his story? There could be some money in it for him.'

'How did you know he was here?' Mrs Torjussen demanded.

'Word gets around,' the journalist said. 'It's not a secret, is it?'

'He's only twelve years old, and he's still trying to get over his experiences. The last thing he needs is people coming here and digging it all up again. I'll thank you to leave him alone.'

'But it's in the public interest,' they complained.

Mrs Torjussen pushed the sitting room door shut so that I couldn't hear any more and she argued with them on the doorstep for some time. When she came back into the room, her face was flushed. 'If you see those men out on the street, just ignore them and walk straight past,' she told me. 'We don't need their sort round here.'

As it happens, I did see them later that day when I went out to meet my friends. They were waiting just round the corner at the bottom of the road.

'Give us a smile, Terry,' the photographer shouted, and so I did. It was a kind of reflex action, but also I was curious. Would they really put me in the newspapers?

A few days later after school I popped in to the newsagent's and was startled to see my own picture looking back at me from the cover of a weekly paper called *Tit-Bits*. 'Terry Smiles Again' read the headline. I started to read the story but it was boring, just explaining that I was the boy whose brother had been killed by the evil Goughs, and that I now lived in Cardiff with foster parents.

Some of the other boys at school saw the story in their parents' newspapers – it had also been in the *Daily Mirror* – and they all started quizzing me about what had happened, looking for sensation and gory details as boys that age will, and I found it all horrible. Mrs Torjussen complained to the editors, I think, but soon other papers knew where I lived and it became fairly common to find a journalist and a photographer waiting to speak to me on my way home from school. It seems the government were putting together a Children's Act that, among other things, would ensure children in state care were properly looked after, and all the newspapers wanted to use my picture to illustrate their stories about it.

Mrs Torjussen used to get very cross. 'They've been hounding that poor boy again today,' I heard her telling her husband when she thought I was in bed. 'I'm sure his brothers must have put them on to us or they'd never have known where to find him. What are we going to do about it?'

'Have you called the council welfare officer? Maybe he could suggest something. We can't go on like this.'

'I'll do that tomorrow,' she said, and I felt a familiar knot of anxiety form. I'd learned not to expect good things to come of it when the council got involved in decisions about my care.

About a week later, I came home from school to find a social worker sitting having a cup of tea with Mrs Torjussen. They looked up as I came in.

'Terry, come and sit down,' Mrs Torjussen said in her kindest voice. 'We need to talk to you ...'

And I knew it was going to be bad news. I just knew. I didn't listen to everything that was said because my ears were buzzing, the way they sometimes did when people were telling me something I didn't want to hear. But I did make out that they wanted me to go and stay in a children's home.

'It won't be for long,' they reassured me, but I knew nothing would ever be the same again. I'd been at the Torjussens' for two years and I'd been happier there than anywhere else I'd ever lived, but now the grown-ups had decided my happiness was to be taken away from me again. I felt betrayed by the Torjussens. It was all I expected of Newport Council, but I thought my 'auntie' and 'uncle' cared more for me than that.

The home I was taken to was only a few streets away in Romilly Road, but the Torjussens didn't visit me there. I suppose they were trying to shake the press off my tail, but at the time I don't remember that being explained to me. It was only a small children's home catering for six children at a time and I became quite friendly with two girls who were roughly the same age as me. They were there because their mum was in hospital and there was no one else to look after them.

I spent six weeks at that home and I felt depressed and defiant in equal measure. Every time I started to trust someone they were taken away from me: the Connops, Joe, Mr Bolton and now the Torjussens. Mrs Torjussen had told me I could stay with her until I left school, found a job and made my own way in life, but then she went back on her word – or so it appeared to me. I was angry with everyone. The only person in the world I could trust was myself. I vowed never to rely on anyone else again.

After six weeks in that home I was returned to the Torjussens', but not for long. In April 1948, at the age of thirteen, I was informed that I was being moved to another children's home a hundred miles away in Birmingham. I'd have to leave my school, my friends and everyone I knew and start from scratch in a new environment. No one explained to me why this was happening. It was yet another commandment handed down by faceless figures of authority, and it completely disrupted my already disturbed education and caused me to lose any trust I had left in human nature.

Chapter Seventeen

Yet again, I was escorted by a Newport Council social worker to a new institution where I was to stay. I was thirteen years old and this was the ninth place I'd been assigned to since I was removed from Bolt Street at the age of five, not counting hospital stays – on average, a new home every year. You'd think I'd be used to it, but I wasn't. On the outside I was sullen and angry, but inside I was depressed, insecure and anxious. Would there be bullies? Would anyone beat me? Was I safe?

In the middle of my first night at St Philip's Boys' Home in Edgbaston, I awoke suddenly from a dream to feel a warm sensation between my legs. Moments later the acrid smell of urine reached my nostrils and I sat bolt upright, my face hot with shame. I had wet myself for the first time in years. Even at the Goughs', with all the terror of daily life, I had never had an accident in bed but now, at the age of thirteen, in the midst of strangers, I had suddenly lost control of my bladder.

My only thought was that I couldn't let any of the other boys find out. I tiptoed to the bathroom and rinsed my pyjama trousers to get rid of the stink, but then I had to put them back on soaking wet because I would have wakened the others if I tried to rifle through my locker in the dark to find a spare pair. I lay there, cold, wet and miserable, and hardly got any sleep for the rest of the night.

Of course, the house mother, whose name was Miss Friend, discovered my little problem the very next morning.

'Goodness! Aren't you a bit old for that?' she exclaimed, while I cringed with embarrassment. She told me that the group of boys who were prone to bed-wetting was roused from sleep at midnight to urinate, and that I would be one of that group from now on. 'You'll be the oldest, though,' she said, tut-tutting, as my cheeks burned crimson and I stared at the floor.

I soon found that St Philip's was a place dominated by rules, which were enforced by Sister Joseph, the Mother Superior, and her staff. The sisters' quarters, kitchen and dining rooms were out of bounds for the boys. There was a playroom where we were allowed to read and draw quietly in the evenings after school, a gymnasium, a music room and a chapel. It was all very strict and no-nonsense and I felt increasingly gloomy as each new rule was explained to me. In the dormitories, the head and legs of the bed had to be arranged in line with the floor-boards, and the beds had to be made up each morning with neatly boxed 'hospital corners'. There were bare floorboards and uniform counterpanes on each bed, and it all felt regimented and institutional.

Miss Friend, the house mother, was an elderly lady with bad legs, who shuffled round in carpet slippers. A week or so after my arrival she took me to consult a doctor in case there was a physical problem causing my lack of bladder control, but he said it was triggered by stress and would clear up in time. I think it only happened two or three more times while I was at St Philip's but it was a source of abject humiliation to me. I hated the midnight wake-up and standing in a queue for the toilet with a group of other, much younger boys who were prone to bed-wetting. None of the boys ever teased me, though. We all had our own problems in there.

One of the nuns who worked there was Sister Gabriel, a cheerful, good-natured nun who had taught me at Croft Castle school, which I attended when I lived with the Connops. It was nice to see a friendly face, but she didn't appear to have heard what had happened to Dennis and I didn't tell her. Talking about it was still too hard. I never told anyone.

There were about twenty boys living in the home and they hovered round me awkwardly at first, but my stamp album broke the ice. One boy asked if he could have a look and a couple of others came over to see what I had and soon we were agreeing swaps and examining each other's albums, so that was OK.

The food was the usual mass-catering stew with soggy vegetables and boiled potatoes. I really missed Mrs Torjussen's cooking. The night before I left we'd had a farewell dinner of chicken and roast potatoes with gravy, then jam sponge and custard for pudding, and I could still remember the rich flavours, which were in stark contrast to this insipid stew.

Bedtime was handled with military precision, each age group following the same procedures: wash, brush teeth, prayers, and so forth. I climbed into bed and tossed and turned for ages, trying to get comfortable on the hard mattress and unyielding pillow.

I was enrolled at the Roman Catholic Oratory School, where the other boys from the home went, and introduced to a strict religious regime. We had to learn the Latin responses parrot-fashion in order to serve Mass in the side altars of the big church. When it was our turn, we were woken at five in the morning and had to walk the half hour up the road to the Oratory Church to serve the six o'clock Mass. On Sundays we served Mass at the High Altar and on those occasions I felt quite proud. I also liked exploring the tunnels of the crypt and lighting the big candles used during the Mass.

I might have been proud to take part in the religious ritual but that didn't stop me mucking around and misbehaving in church. We sneaked in comics to read during long boring services, we carved our names in candle wax, and made fun of the doddery old priests. One of the priests, Father Frank, was in charge of disciplining boys at the Home, and he had a painful, nasty method of chastising us, which I was introduced to before long.

Five boys, including me, were taken aside at bedtime and led into Father Frank's office. He was wearing his cassock and looked very stern. A single chair stood in the middle of the room.

'Stand facing the wall,' he instructed us. 'O'Neill, you come forwards first.'

I walked over to him, my mouth dry and palms sweating. I expected him to have a cane, but all I could see was a big wooden bath brush resting by the wall.

'Lower your pyjama trousers and kneel in front of the chair,' he ordered, so I did as he said, and I couldn't help trembling as an image flashed into my head of Dennis naked and bent over the pig bench. 'Now hold on to the seat of the chair and raise your knees off the ground.'

I pushed up, resting my weight on my hands and toes, thrusting my buttocks into the air, and seconds later I yelped as the bath brush swing down onto one buttock then the other. I felt a tingling sensation, like pins and needles. Father Frank paced round the room reading quotations from his Bible and after he had finished a circuit he stopped, put the Bible down, and whacked me again, once on each buttock. This time it really stung and I cried out in pain. Off he went, walking slowly round the room reading his Bible, then he stopped to give me two more blows. The area was so sensitized that these last smacks were agonizing and I screamed out loud. The other four lads standing facing the wall could hear everything that was going on but couldn't see what was happening and it must have been horrible for them to know it was their turn next.

After I'd had my six whacks, I was sent to bed. I lay face down, because my buttocks were too sore to lie on my back, and listened as the remaining boys were punished in Father Frank's room. It was a strange ritual, and one that I was to be a victim of on several occasions because no matter how much I might resolve to avoid it in future, my defiant streak always came to the fore. I was angry that I had been sent there, angry and resentful, and I had a kind of 'what the hell' attitude. It was sore, but nothing like as painful as the stripes I'd had to put up with at the Goughs' and I developed a 'tough guy' persona as a kind of shield.

I became close to three boys in particular – Spam, Ian and John. Spam got his nickname from the initials of his real name, Albert May, preceded by St Philip's. He was a cheerful sort and a great pal to me. Ian sang soprano in the church choir and was fantastic at art. John was the joker of the pack, always trying to make us laugh. The three of us were always together and often up to mischief, but I was probably the ringleader and it was usually me who got the blame. I'd got a reputation by then. I wasn't the dutiful, respectful Catholic boy they hoped to produce at that home; the indoctrination wasn't working.

In contrast to life at the Torjussens', I had hardly any free time now. Evenings after school were spent in the playroom reading quietly (or getting into trouble if we messed around). On Saturday mornings we had to clean the home from top to bottom, each boy having a particular job allocated after breakfast. Sometimes we had to rub polish on the dormitory floors and polish them to a high shine with a heavy, long-handled polisher. We wore thick padded cloths on our feet and slid around the rooms as if on a skating rink, to avoid making any scuff marks on the shiny surface, then we had to put the beds back in their regimental lines. All the banisters had to be polished and surfaces dusted, and the chores usually kept us busy through till lunchtime.

After lunch we'd be given our pocket money – sixpence for the older lads and threepence for the youngsters, which we could spend on sweets in the tuck shop. On Saturday afternoons us older boys were allowed to go for a walk in the city centre and look around the shops, but it frustrated me not having much money to spend. I talked to Father Frank and he arranged for me to get a couple of paying jobs in the monastery. I helped with the gardening, which I enjoyed, and I also manned the main door to the priests' house at weekends. If callers came for any of the priests, I had to contact them using a blow-pipe system on the wall. Each priest had his own whistle and when I sounded it, he knew to come down and see his visitor. I was paid ten shillings for a day's work at this, but it was put into a savings account for me rather than given to me to spend. I would have done anything for money. It was my safety net. As long as I had some cash, no one could ever starve me again, and if things got too bad, I'd have enough money to run away.

When the summer holidays came, the Torjussens arrived to pick me up and take me off for a couple of weeks to the Pembroke coast, staying with Mrs Torjussen's mother. It was strange seeing them again. I still felt cross with them for sending me away, so there wasn't the relaxed, happy atmosphere there had been before, but I enjoyed the holiday nonetheless. I especially liked going to the fish market where fishermen auctioned their catch of the day. These weather-blasted, rugged men spoke rapidly in a kind of code, and the bidders raised a finger or simply tipped their heads to make a bid. I liked the fishy smell and looking round at all the glassy-eyed, slippery creatures with beautiful silvery colours.

One evening, Mrs Torjussen mentioned to me that she had contacted Newport Council to ask them for news of Freddie.

'He's still staying at the Pickerings,' she told me, 'and going to your old school. I think he's very happy there.'

'Why did you want to get in touch with him?' I asked.

She pursed her mouth quickly. 'I'd thought he might like to join us on holiday, so that you and he could be reunited. But he didn't want to. I think he probably doesn't want to be reminded of things. It must have been tough for him as well.'

Not as tough as for me, I thought. But I understood. It was easier to keep that whole period and all those memories locked up in a box. I wasn't sure whether I wanted to see Freddie myself. It would have brought back too many things I wasn't ready to think about. It would have taken me back to that summer when we used to play in the pond in the churchyard and build dams across the stream, back before it had all gone bad.

I spent my fourteenth birthday in St Philip's, and the whole of the following year as well. I got into the routine of the home, but I still found myself in trouble frequently, mostly due to my youthful high spirits. There was one occasion when I pretended to flush a friend's head down the toilet for a laugh; I just pushed his head down and pulled the flush, it didn't wet so much as a hair on his head. As far as the nuns were concerned, though, you'd think I'd desecrated the holy cross or blasphemed in the name of the Virgin Mary so great was the fuss. It happened at school and the headmaster punished me with a stroke of the cane on each hand, which was fine because my hands were still so roughened from the stripes I'd had at the Goughs' that I barely had any sensation left on my palms. But then Sister Joseph decided that wasn't nearly enough punishment for the scale of the crime and Father Frank was called to do duty with his bath brush – six of the best on my bare buttocks. I hated that punishment. It was painful and degrading at the same time. I'd reached an age when I didn't feel an older man should be seeing my naked bottom; there was something about it that didn't feel right. And it never failed to make me remember poor Dennis naked and tied over the pig bench.

I didn't have long to go at the school, as my fifteenth birthday was approaching. Whenever anyone asked what I wanted to do, I always said I wanted to be a farmer. I enjoyed working with animals and growing things, and I liked being out in the open air. For a while I considered emigrating to Australia under something called the 'Big Brother' scheme, whereby the Australian authorities paid your fare out there and guaranteed to set you up. An Australian woman called Molly Shortt had been writing and sending food parcels to me since I was at Besford House (I particularly loved the jars of peanut butter she sent). She urged me to try living in Australia and Newport Council said they would support me, but Mrs Torjussen talked me out of it because it was so far away. If I got into a bad situation out there I wouldn't have anyone to turn to for help, while at least in our area I could go to the Torjussens if I was in trouble. I wouldn't ever live with them again, but they still took an interest in me and assured me they would help if I needed them.

One Saturday when I was walking in town, I noticed there a community exhibition about places of local interest and decided to have a look around. At one stall there was a film showing about a Catholic priest called John Bosco, born near Turin in Italy, who had formed an order called the Salesians. As a young boy, his family was very poor and he spent his time working on the land and looking after their few cows and sheep. When he grew up he trained as a priest and moved to Turin, where he spent his days roaming the streets and looking after young boys who were hungry, homeless or in trouble. He converted an old barn into a workshop and trained these boys in different trades so they could earn their own living, using teaching methods based on love and kindness rather than fear and punishment. He said that education was a matter of the heart, and that it was important for boys to be loved and to know that they were loved.

I sat mesmerized throughout the film. The story of this extraordinary man was heart-warming and I wished I could have been one of his apprentices, just to be close to him. He had died in 1888 but his disciples set up Salesian schools and colleges round the world to carry on his good work. I walked back to the home, feeling very moved by what I had heard.

Shortly after that, just before my fifteenth birthday, a social worker came from Newport Council to have a chat with me about my future. He said that because I had expressed an interest in farming, they had found a place for me at an agricultural college in Gloucestershire, where I could be taken in as a boarder and trained in farming. I would be starting on 9 January 1950.

'That's great!' I said. 'Thanks very much.' I was delighted to be getting away from St Philip's, with all its petty rules and Father Frank's bath brush.

The college where I was enrolled was called Blaisdon Hall. It wasn't until I arrived there that I found out that it was run by the 'Salesian Order of John of Bosco'. What a strange coincidence! Because of that, I had a good feeling about Blaisdon right from the start. Maybe I would be treated as an adult now and would no longer feel so vulnerable and insecure. I could start making my own decisions instead of having faceless officials at Newport Council determine my fate.

Chapter Eighteen

Blaisdon Hall was near the Forest of Dean in the Vale of Gloucestershire, about a mile's walk from a railway station. I was impressed by the first view of it, at the end of a snaking tarmac drive. It was huge, with lots of turrets and fancy architecture, even posher-looking than the Connops' house. I was greeted by a twinkly-eyed priest in black robes: 'Terry O'Neill?' he asked. 'We've got something in common already. My name's Father O'Neill!'

Once the social worker who had accompanied me left, Father O'Neill showed me round my new home, a tour that was to take a couple of hours because it was so big. It was then he told me it was a Salesian order, and seemed impressed that I had heard of John Bosco and knew about his work. The ground floor, with oak-panelled walls throughout, had a dining room, offices, visiting room and living rooms, and an ornate staircase that led to the upper floors. My dormitory was on the top floor, with a view out to the sprawling farm behind the house. I could see rows of stables and milking sheds and a paddock, and beyond that several cultivated fields, all surrounded by forest stretching almost as far as the eye could see. From my lofty viewpoint I could see boys hard at work, tending the animals, digging the gardens or driving a tractor round the yard, the whole scene lit by pale January sunshine. I felt a warmth inside me. I had a strong feeling I was going to like it here.

The day started with Mass, followed by a hearty breakfast (often bacon and eggs) and our cleaning chores, which everyone joined in. After that we went to the training area to which we'd been allocated. I was disappointed when Father O'Neill told me they were starting me off in the carpentry shop.

'I want to be a farmer,' I complained. 'I thought that's what I was here for.'

'It's a good training, being able to work a piece of wood. Don't sniff at it,' he told me. 'You'll get on to the farming all in good time.'

In fact I soon found that I enjoyed learning about the nature of the wood, cutting and smoothing, working with the grain, and making my creations as perfect as I could. There was a cold snap that February and I realized I'd probably done well to be working indoors in that weather, but as spring arrived and there was heat in the sun once more, I yearned to be out in the fields.

Brother McAvoy, who ran the carpentry workshop, told me that I could move on as soon as I made him a perfect miniature five-barred farm gate. I had to cut, joint and glue it to his satisfaction, a task that took me the best part of a week, but at last he declared himself pleased with my work, and told me that I was being transferred to the gardening section.

I spent six weeks in the vegetable gardens, learning how to plant, weed and harvest the different crops. They tried to teach me the Latin names for plants and flowers but I couldn't pronounce them and I'm afraid they never stuck in my head. Still I worked hard, enjoying being out in the open air, and after six weeks I was finally moved to the farming section, where I had wanted to be all along.

Father Dan, the priest in charge of farming, was an affable man who was popular with all the boys. He supervised us with the help of a team of lay brothers, dedicated men who lived like priests but were not ordained. There was a lot to learn and I threw myself into it with enthusiasm. My first job was milking the cows and then hand-feeding the newborn calves from a bottle. The older calves could drink from a bucket that I tipped up for them. I couldn't help thinking about the day when Mrs Gough had locked me in the cubby-hole for spilling some milk as I fed a calf, but the memory passed quickly because the brothers at Blaisdon Hall couldn't have been more different from the Goughs. They were smiling, encouraging, friendly, and no one ever got punished there to my knowledge.

We were given a lot of freedom while being expected to do our jobs to the best of our ability, and I flourished in that kind of environment. There was nothing to rebel against. The food was good and plentiful; the other boys were all there for the same reason as me – because they wanted to learn about farming – so we got on and helped each other. There was no sense of competitiveness. Farming, I learned, is all about cooperation. Once we finished our tasks, we were free to go back to the Hall at five o'clock but we tended to stay behind and help anyone else who hadn't finished their work.

As well as cows, they had pigs, chickens and horses at Blaisdon. I didn't work at the stud farm but I liked watching the horses galloping round the field and I learned about the care of all the animals from watching the tasks the other boys did. For example, I learned that they kept a virus-free atmosphere for the chickens by moving the coops onto fresh grass every day. I learned that you make silage by compressing grass into bales in the spring and summer months so that you have enough to feed cattle in winter. I learned about the way you rotate the crops to different fields year on year. It was all fascinating to me and I drank it in.

When I got to bed at night, I fell asleep within seconds of my head hitting the pillow. Not once did I wet the bed at Blaisdon Hall. Not once did I waken screaming after one of my awful nightmares. I was simply too tired. Something else as well: I was too happy.

Of course, I still messed around from time to time. My mischievous reputation wasn't for nothing. The need to take great care when using farm machinery, particularly tractors, had been hammered home from the start, but one day a group of us began messing around while we were making silage. We'd dug a deep pit and were filling it with grass cut from the fields. As it got fuller, one boy had to drive a tractor over the top to compress it. The fuller it got, the more the tractor jumped around like a bucking bronco, tipping right back as it drove over the bulging heap. We started a race to see who could rake up their next load from a field and get it back to the pit fastest. I was going great guns and threw my load in and was tamping it down with the rake held upside down, when the chap driving the tractor reversed over it. There was a loud hissing sound as one of the prongs burst a big tractor tyre.

We all stopped and looked at each other nervously.

'What the hell did you think you were doing?' the tractor driver yelled at me.

'Why the hell didn't you look where you were going?' I yelled back. 'And more to the point, what are we going to tell Father Dan?'

We were busy trying to invent an excuse when Father Dan came charging down the field, having seen the whole thing. I tensed. Would I be caned? Or hit with a bath brush? I was so used to beatings when I did something wrong that I was sure I was going to get one now, but instead Father Dan gave us an ear-bashing.

'What have I said about taking care when operating farm machinery? It could have been a boy under the wheels of that tractor instead of a rake, the load of you were mucking around so much. This isn't a children's playground. It's a working environment.'

We stared at the ground feeling stupid because, of course, everything he said was true. They treated us as grown-ups at Blaisdon and expected us to behave that way, and we'd let him down. I felt really bad about it.

Not long after this incident, I had a narrow scrape during the hay harvest. About six boys were using their pitchforks to toss the hay up to me and another boy who were standing on top of the trailer. Just as we drove past the railings separating the farm from the church-yard, the tractor lurched, the bed of the trailer came away from the chassis, and the two of us on top were hurled through the air. My companion landed on a grave in the churchyard, where he was winded but not hurt. They found me hanging upside down from the railings as if on a trapeze, because my knees had got trapped between loops. I was shaken up and had to rest for a few hours, but it could have been a lot worse. It was a reminder, if I had needed one, of the myriad dangers of farming.

Our work changed with the seasons: muck-raking, harrowing, grass-seeding, potato planting, threshing the corn, or working with the animals. When potato-harvesting time came, they asked for volunteers. It was back-breaking work but there was never any shortage of boys signing up because you got paid sixpence a sack. I always liked earning my own money so I was at the front of the queue.

Each summer while I was at Blaisdon, we were sent for a long summer holiday in Porthcawl, on the South Wales coast. The first time, I went ahead with an advance party in the trucks carrying our equipment and helped to set up camp, erecting the tents and building a huge cooking pit where we would make the evening meals. For the first two weeks we did army cadet training on the sand dunes, getting instruction on map reading and practising our marching, but after that we were on holiday proper and could mess around on the beach all day. At last I learned to swim, and I spent my days either in the water or clambering around the rock pools looking for crabs, jellyfish and starfish. In the evenings we went to the fairground, played board games in our tents, or listened to the 'cats' whiskers' wireless sets a couple of boys had brought, with the aerials connected to our tent poles to aid reception. One lad even had a wind-up gramophone and a few old Bakelite records.

These were innocent, happy times, when I began to feel 'normal' again. The brothers knew about my background but none of the boys did, and I liked it that way. There were a few reminders of the Goughs as I trained to be a farmer, but the brothers dealt with every problem with wisdom and fairness and were never cruel. I felt sad around the anniversary of Dennis's death in early January – it came upon me like a lead weight, even if I hadn't consciously remembered the date – and each year I just had to wait quietly and keep myself to myself until it passed.

In March 1951, I realized that Mr Gough would have served his six years in jail and, chances were, he would be released soon if he hadn't been already. It was horrible to imagine him walking the streets again as a free man but I decided not to think about it. I'd put it in the box at the back of my head. I was far enough away from Shrewsbury that there was virtually no chance of ever bumping into him.

That October, as my seventeenth birthday approached, the brothers decided I had done enough basic training and they found me a job on a farm near Pontypool in Gwent, on a month's trial. I was sorry to leave Blaisdon but excited that I would have a proper job, earning a salary; I still equated money with safety.

Once again a Newport social worker accompanied me on the journey, by train and then a walk up a hill. When we arrived, the farmer explained that I would be paid the standard agricultural wage of the day, which was three pounds, seventeen shillings and threepence a week. From that he would deduct fourteen shillings and sixpence a week for my board and lodgings and two shillings, eleven pence for National Insurance contributions. The social worker told me I'd be allowed to keep ten shillings a week as pocket money and they would bank the rest to save for my future. Until I turned eighteen, the council could still make these decisions for me.

The farm was small, but I lived as family with the farmer and his wife and two young children. I was up at the crack of dawn milking the cows before breakfast. After that, I was kept busy sterilizing the milking utensils, cleaning out the cowsheds, feeding and tending the sheep, chickens and pigs, then at three o'clock in the afternoon, I had to get the cows in for the afternoon milking and clean everything again before tea. It was a tiring day but I loved working with animals and I was happy there, so I was delighted when, after my month's trial, the farmer said he was willing to keep me on.

Because the farm was so remote, I realized I'd need a bicycle if I ever wanted to go anywhere on my days off and I wrote to Newport Council asking if they could release some money to me for this purpose. I knew that as well as the savings from my wages, they had all the money that had been sent to me by the public after the newspaper reports of Dennis's death and my treatment by the Goughs. After a brief delay, a social worker turned up with some cash and took me to a bicycle shop in Newport where I picked out a shiny new bike. I felt very proud of myself as I cycled all the way back to Pontypool. It gave me the freedom to cycle over to Mass on Sundays, and to get down to the cinema in town, which had previously meant a bus ride plus a long walk.

A couple of times during my stay on the farm, I had a strange otherworldly type of experience. I suppose it was due to the isolation as much as anything else. The first thing that happened was one night when I was coming back from the cinema at about ten-thirty on a very dark night. I decided to take a shortcut across a field and was just climbing a stile when I heard a loud whooshing sound that seemed to be coming straight towards me from behind a hedge. The hairs on the back of my neck stood up and I rushed at top speed to the far side of the field then leapt a stile to get back to the farmhouse. Next morning when I visited the spot, I decided the noise had probably been caused by a cow I'd disturbed on the other side of the hedge and I put it out of my mind.

Not long afterwards, the milk marketing inspector turned up one morning looking utterly petrified, his face white as a sheet. He said that as he opened the gates at a level crossing down the hill he had seen someone standing beside his car, so he offered them a lift up the road. He closed the gates behind him, came back to the car, and the person had vanished. There was no one there, and nowhere anyone could have gone. He was in quite a state about it.

And then one night I woke up and saw a misty form in my bedroom. I was startled but for some reason I wasn't scared of it, even though I knew it must be a spirit. It was a benign, calm presence and I could tell it didn't mean me any harm. After that I kept having visits from this spirit periodically and in my head I called it Charlie. I didn't realize at first, but I became convinced later that it was Dennis, coming back to check up on me. I could feel a sense of his equanimity. At any rate, the visits were immensely comforting. I didn't tell anyone else about them, of course. I didn't want to get a reputation for being queer in the head.

After I'd been at the farm for about six months, I asked the farmer if I could have a day off to go back and visit my friends at Blaisdon Hall, and he agreed. It was fifty miles away and took me over three hours to get there, but it was great to see everyone again and they all made a big fuss of me, asking for details of my life in Pontypool. During the course of the conversation, Brother Joe asked what the farmer was paying me. In my innocence, I replied, 'Two pounds', forgetting about the stoppages for my board and lodgings, which made it up to the standard wage.

'What is that farmer playing at? You should be getting much more than that. He's taking advantage of you, so he is!'

Brother Joe contacted the Newport authorities to complain and I wished I hadn't opened my mouth. I was happy at the farm and didn't want to cause trouble. A few weeks later, though, a social worker came from Newport to tell the farmer that he would have to pay me more, and it was the beginning of the end. He became very grumpy with me and began to find fault with my work, which up till then he had been quite happy with. I was allergic to criticism so we had a big row one morning and I stormed off, grabbing my bike and cycling all the way to Newport, where I knocked on the door of a children's home I knew of in Chepstow Road.

'I can't stay at that farm any more,' I complained. 'The farmer is totally unreasonable.'

A social worker tried to smooth things over for me, but suggested I went back to Blaisdon Hall for a couple of weeks' break, and while I was there, Father Dan asked if I would like to stay on and work on the farm as an old boy, helping them to supervise the youngsters. I didn't need to be asked twice. I collected my belongings from Pontypool, where I made things up with the farmer and left on good terms, then I went back to Blaisdon, where I lived happily until my army call-up papers arrived just after my eighteenth birthday.

I could have asked to defer my National Service because I worked on the land, but I was looking forward to joining up. In the army I would learn how to defend myself properly, and I never knew when I might need that. I particularly hoped it would give me a chance to travel overseas, as far away from England as possible. I went for the medical, which I passed, and a couple of weeks later I was told to report to Blackdown Camp in Surrey to begin my training in February 1953. One adventure was over and another was about to begin.

Chapter Nineteen

When I turned up at Blackdown Camp, lots of the other new recruits were quaking with nerves, as it was the first time they had left home. I was fine, though. I'd had plenty of practice in arriving at a new place and learning the ropes, and I had no 'home' to miss.

We were taken to the quartermaster's stores, where there was pandemonium while they tried to find everyone uniforms that fitted and hand out the correct pieces of kit. We hobbled around in over-sized or under-sized vests, pants and boots, laughing at the sight of each other, and it took a full day to get us all sorted. The next day it was time for the cruel short-back-and-sides haircuts, and we were given a variety of vaccinations that made our arms stiffen up.

I got through the basic training without any problems, although I didn't enjoy the NCOs yelling at us from morning till night and calling us all kinds of names. I had to bite my tongue to stop myself shouting back. At the end of the first six weeks, they said that if we changed from the two-year national service contract to a three-year regular soldier's one, our weekly pay would increase to two pounds a week. I gave it a bit of thought and decided to accept the offer. Why not? I had nothing to lose.

Next, we were given a choice of skills in which the army would train us. I was told it was virtually impossible to be trained as a driver because there were no vacancies, but that's what I set my heart on and somehow I managed to wangle it – possibly because I'd signed up as a 'regular'; possibly because on my application form I'd written 'driving' in both the first choice and the second choice box. I loved the feeling of being behind the wheel and managed to pass the very tricky military driving test on my second attempt, while most people needed several tries.

Now that we had qualified, we were all desperate to find out where our postings would be. The first clue came when lightweight clothing and strips of cloth called puttees were distributed. The puttees, we were told, should be wrapped round the tops of our boots to stop scorpions getting in. Scorpions! That meant we were going somewhere hot and exotic. Our commanding officer confirmed that it would be 'somewhere in the Middle East' and I was delighted. The further the better, as far as I was concerned.

We set sail from Southampton on a ship called the *Empire Fowey*, and I had a moment of sadness at embarkation when all the other lads lined up to wave goodbye to their families on the quayside. There was no one for me to wave to, no one who particularly cared what happened to me out there. The Torjussens still kept in touch, and I'd been told I was always welcome back at Blaisdon Hall, but none of my own family had made the effort to contact me since the brief visit from Tom and Charlie six years earlier. I was totally alone in the world, with no ties. Life would be whatever I made it.

In June 1953, we landed at Port Said in Egypt and caught the train down to Fayid, a remote, dusty, scorching RAF airbase by the Suez Canal where I was to spend the next two and a half years. Most of the time I was on transport duty, driving trucks to collect food rations from the supply depot or ferrying men to and from the port or the airport. In summer the heat was blistering and I spent most of my free time in the camp's swimming pool. At night it was hard to sleep, with bedbugs, mosquitoes and a temperature that could still be oppressive after the sun went down. There wasn't much to do when I was off-duty. There was a cinema in town that we could visit of an evening, or a bar in the NAAFI, but during the first year in Egypt I had no interest in drinking. I tried it a couple of times but didn't like the taste.

However, one night I got into a bad state of mind. I was bored, I was lonely, and sometimes I got angry with no one in particular, about nothing I could put my finger on. Anger took over and made me behave in ways that were otherwise out of character. I had a drink or two then caught the army bus into town and roamed the market stalls looking for trouble. I was supposed to be meeting a friend but he was late, so I had another drink or two and when my friend turned up I picked a fight with him. He won, mainly because he wasn't under the influence, and he left me lying by the roadside, whereupon I missed the last bus back to base. The military policemen on duty didn't report me, though.

'He looks as though he's been punished enough already,' one quipped, looking at my bruised eye and cut lip.

It was the first time my behaviour was adversely influenced by alcohol like that – but it wouldn't be the last. I discovered that when the demons in my head started chattering too loudly, I could buy myself a few hours of anaesthesia by drinking alcohol. It was a way of running away from my memories, my loneliness and my anger. Whenever the Goughs came into my thoughts, I knew I could always turn to beer to help me deal with the horrible visions and a feeling of utter, helpless fury that came over me.

Rather than angry, though, I spent most of the time in Fayid bored out of my skull, and my old mischievousness got me into trouble a few times. I spent twenty-eight days in the nick for stealing food from the stores and stashing it in my locker. It's not that we were under-fed; maybe it was just force of habit to stockpile food. I never wanted to go short again, the way I had been at the Goughs'. I needed a safety net and this was my way of constructing one, although it wasn't very well thought through because when the shortages were noticed I was the first suspect and the evidence was easy to find!

About halfway through my service in Egypt, a letter arrived for me. I looked at the Newport postmark and decided it must be from the council – but the address was handwritten and it didn't look like an official letter. I tore it open and was amazed to find a note from my sister Rose. She said she had tracked me down with the help of Newport Council because she wanted to find out how I was doing and give me her address. She said that Mam had remarried since Dad died, and that they all lived near each other in Wilson Street, Pillgwenlly. Bully for you, I thought. I had very little interest in them so I didn't bother replying to Rose. What was there to say after all? I kept her letter, though.

At last, in January 1956, my tour of duty was over and I was flown home, my first experience of flying. I gazed out through the tiny window at the propellers whirring around until they became a blur. It was night-time but I watched as we passed over desert, mountains and ocean, looking at the lights dotted on the ground below and wondering what life would have in store for me next.

Where would I stay? My three years in the army had come to an end so what would I do to earn my living?

When we landed in England, snow lay thick on the ground, which was very welcome to me after two and a half years of seeing nothing but sand. It was good to feel cold again instead of sweltering in the heat. I waited in camp for a few days while my demob papers were sorted out, then I was issued with civvies – a suit, a hat and a pair of shoes – along with a rail warrant, which was supposed to take me to my home town. But where was my 'home town'? There was no clear-cut answer to that question.

I went to Blaisdon Hall for a couple of weeks to catch up with old friends there, and I thought about looking for another farming job, like the one I'd had at Pontypool, but it was such hard work for so little pay that I'd gone off the idea. I still loved the outdoors but the driving job I'd had in the army had been a much easier way to earn a living than getting up at the crack of dawn to milk cows. I had an idea that I would like to become a long-distance lorry driver because I'd enjoy the freedom of being my own boss rather than answering to someone who kept peering over my shoulder. How would I get started in that kind of career though? On a whim, I decided to go to Newport and investigate what I'd have to do to get into that line of work. I arranged to stay at a children's reception home there for a couple of weeks, just till I found my feet.

The day after I arrived in Newport, I went out for a walk. I crossed the River Usk and in the distance I could see the Transporter Bridge on which I had ridden as a little boy. There it was, the two towers and the long gondola raised high above the water. It was a real trip down memory lane. I stood and watched for a while as it carried some cars across the river, then I wandered towards Commercial Road, where I had lived once. I walked down past Bolt Street, the last home I'd lived in with my blood family before the council took us away, and all kinds of memories were suddenly flooding my head – memories from way back, when Dennis and I hung out down at the docks, playing hopscotch and throwing stones in the water. I had a strong pang of missing him that brought a wave of sadness.

Suddenly, I got an overpowering sense that Dennis's spirit was with me. I could feel him nearby, watching me, as if there was something he wanted me to do. Instinctively, I reached into the inside pocket of my jacket and pulled out my sister Rose's letter: the address she gave was number 9, Wilson Street.

'Can you direct me to Wilson Street?' I asked a middle-aged woman with a shopping bag.

She put her bag down and thought carefully. 'Your best way is to take a left into Portland Street, then a right into Castle Street and it will be the second – no, the third road on the left.'

That was right down almost at the river's edge. 'Thank you, ma'am.'

My feet slowed as I approached the house. Did I really want to do this? What was the point? But it felt as though there was unfinished business there, so I knocked on the door of number 9, feeling more nervous than I'd felt for a long time.

The door opened and a middle-aged blonde woman stood in the doorway.

'Sorry to trouble you,' I said. 'I'm looking for the O'Neill family and I wondered if they still live here?'

The woman peered at me suspiciously for a moment or two then her face lit up. 'Terry? Our Terry? It's Betty, your sister Betty.'

I wouldn't have recognized her in a month of Sundays. I couldn't even remember what she'd looked like nearly twenty years earlier.

'Mam?' she yelled over her shoulder. 'You'll never guess who's here.' To me, she said 'Come in, come in,' and stepped back to let me past her into the narrow hallway that led down to their back room.

My mam was sitting at the table with an elderly gent. 'Terry, is it really you? I knew you'd come back to us. I always knew it!' She gave me a big hug, which made me feel very embarrassed and uncomfortable. 'This is my husband,' she told me, pointing to the elderly gent, so I shook hands with him.

Betty went into the kitchen to get us all a cup of tea and Mam kept chatting away, exclaiming how well I looked with my deep tan from Egypt, and how tall I'd got, and so on. I just felt shy. I found a seat over by the window that looked out into a bare back yard and took the cup of tea Betty handed me and barely said a word.

Mam explained that she and her new husband were living with Betty and her husband and son. I didn't have much to say in return after explaining I was just back from military service. They made up for it, though, telling me all the local gossip and news about the rest of the family.

'Guess what I've got?' Betty suddenly exclaimed. She rushed through to the front room and came back holding a framed photograph that she passed to me. I caught my breath when I looked at it. There were the three of us, Dennis, Freddie and me, standing in the garden at the Connops'. We were so young, without a care in the world. Freddie was shielding his eyes from the sun so you couldn't see him so clearly and I'm looking sideways, but Dennis is smiling straight at the camera, looking happy and healthy and just like his old self. I got goosebumps all over, and fought against tears springing to my eyes. God, how I missed him!

I had a lump in my throat so my voice was all husky as I asked, 'Where did you get this?'

'I wrote to Newport Council asking if they had a picture and, ages later, this arrived. It's lovely, isn't it? We'll have to make you a copy.'

'I'd like that,' I said, clutching it. I didn't want to hand it back again. It was very emotional seeing Dennis his old self, as opposed to the memories I had of him in the last weeks at the Goughs'. It sent me back inside myself, into the dark place inside my head that I tried my best to block off.

Betty was talking nineteen to the dozen, so I forced my attention back to her voice. She told me that most of the family lived nearby except Freddie, who as far as they knew was still up in the Shrewsbury area, and Tom, who had become the superintendent of a children's home in Kent, where he lived with his wife and two sons.

News of my arrival spread and soon the sitting room was full: Cyril, Charles and Rose popped in, along with their children and partners, whose names I was told and promptly forgot. Everyone was talking at once, telling me about their lives, and I felt totally overwhelmed. These people were strangers to me but they all thought differently. They wanted to be part of my life story, with all its twists and turns. Dennis's name wasn't mentioned but he was the elephant in the room, the one thing no one wanted to talk about. I certainly didn't.

'What are your plans now you've left the army?' Rose asked. 'Are you staying here in Newport?'

I told them about my idea of becoming a long-distance truck driver, and said I had no idea where I would eventually settle, that I was just in Newport to test the lie of the land.

'Come and stay with us for a bit,' Betty urged. 'We want to get to know you again. You're our own flesh and blood.'

I agreed to stay because it seemed rude not to. They put me in a little upstairs room, which I think was usually Betty's son's bedroom, meaning he had to sleep on the sofa. The day after my arrival I got a job working as a tyre-fitter in a garage a couple of streets away – I just walked up, introduced myself, and asked if they needed a hand. I told myself it was only a temporary stop-gap, but in fact I soon came to enjoy it. It was hard work but I liked my boss, Mr Alford, who treated me like his own son, often inviting me to visit his family in Chepstow. I was given my own van and sometimes had to drive over to the firm's Cardiff depot to help out there. They seemed to trust me and appreciate the work I was doing, and that felt good.

I'd decided to move to the Cardiff branch and had arranged digs for myself there when something happened that would change my mind. A young woman called Pat Ryan came to work as an assistant to Mr Alford's secretary and right from the first day she caught my eye. She was slim and pretty with brown curly hair and she dressed in tight skirts with high-heeled shoes. Whenever I had to go into the office for anything, I'd start blushing like an idiot. I'd try to turn my back so she didn't see my beetroot-red complexion, but that looked even worse. I'm sure she knew I was embarrassed because I fancied her and she tried to help me out of my misery by being friendly, but I had no experience with girls and didn't know how to start chatting back. What should I say?

I broke the ice by offering to give her a lift home after work one night when it was pouring with rain, and she invited me in to meet her family and have a cup of tea. After that I started to give her a lift home most days and began to feel a little more comfortable with her. I was still painfully shy but she was chatty and made me feel that it was all right if I didn't keep up my end of the conversation.

My move to Cardiff was all arranged by this stage and I had to go through with it, but within three weeks I decided that I missed Pat. I asked if I could reverse my decision and Mr Alford agreed. I came back to Newport and moved in as a lodger with a foreman tyre-fitter and his family because I didn't want to impose on Betty any longer. And finally I asked Pat if she would like to come out to the cinema one night; to my amazement she said yes.

Growing up in all-male environments, I'd thought girls were an alien species who only talked about clothes and feminine things, but I found Pat incredibly easy to talk to. I told her all about my time in Egypt and about training as a farmer at Blaisdon Hall, and then one day, when we had been seeing each other for a few weeks, to my great surprise I found myself telling her about Dennis's and my experiences on Bank Farm. She had tears in her eyes through most of my story and she was sobbing when I described waking up in the morning and not being able to rouse Dennis.

'I remember when I was a little girl and wouldn't eat my tea, my mam would say to me that I was lucky to have a good meal in front of me, because there were two little boys who had been starved by a farmer and his wife and that one of them died. I can't believe that was you and your brother!'

I described to her all the details of the way I found out from the man in the hospital that Dennis was dead, and then the court case and the Goughs' sentences and she was warm and sympathetic and said all the right things. It was the first time I'd ever told anyone about it and it felt good to get it off my chest.

'Where is he buried?' she asked, and I told her that to the best of my knowledge he was in St Woolos cemetery.

'Why don't we go and find his grave?'

I looked at her, and it was at that moment I knew for sure I was falling in love with this wonderful girl. She seemed to care so deeply about what had happened to me that I found it easy to talk to her about it all. There was nothing I couldn't say. I felt a bond with her. I realized she was the first person I had trusted since Dennis himself.

'I'd like that,' I said.

Pat told me there was a small Catholic chapel in the cemetery where they kept a record of the burials. However, when we got there it was locked and there was no one nearby we could ask. We went for a walk round the cemetery, with its higgledy-piggledy gravestones;

some were ancient and overgrown with moss, while others were bright and new, with fresh flowers in pretty vases. We tried to work out if there was a system, and if we might find a section with January 1945 graves somewhere, but they seemed quite random in their organization.

Our walk took us in a circle back to the chapel and I went over to try the door again. This time, to my surprise, it opened. Inside there was a table with a single drawer, and within that there was a book. I picked it up and opened it at random, and the first entry on the page the book opened at read: 'Dennis O'Neill', with the grave number.

'Oh my gosh!' I exclaimed in shock.

It wasn't the last coincidence of the day, though. As we walked towards Dennis's grave, we passed two women who were tending another grave and one of them looked up.

'Excuse me,' she said. 'Is your name O'Neill?'

'Yes.'

'When I saw you walking around, I thought for a moment it was our Jack,' she said. 'Jack O'Neill.'

'He was my dad,' I replied.

'We're your aunties, in that case, your dad's sisters. I'm Lil and this is Gin.'

'I'm Terry,' I said, 'and this is my girlfriend, Pat.'

I saw Lil and Gin give each other a quick glance – that look I sometimes saw people give each other when they realized who I was. 'Oh, he's the one …' it said. We chatted for a while then they gave us directions to the row of graves where Dennis was buried along with my father.

Pat and I had to walk up and down the row several times before we found the correct grave, because there was no headstone or marking on it, only a metal plate with a number. Long grass grew up around it and some kind of prickly bramble had twisted its way across, sinking in deep roots. I saw a cemetery attendant and ran over to confirm that this was, indeed, Dennis's grave. I just stared at the spot, as if somehow I would be able to see through the soil to where he lay. Pat got down on her knees and started tearing up the bramble.

'We should come back with some shears to trim the grass, and bring some flowers next time,' Pat said.

A funny feeling came over me and I knew then and there that she was the woman I wanted to marry. She was totally on my side. It was a feeling I wasn't used to, but she was so straightforward and caring that I knew I could trust her with anything. I knew I had to somehow persuade this woman to spend the rest of her life with me but I felt incredibly shy about it.

Finally I just blurted it out one day as I was dropping her off outside her house.

'I've been thinking it might be … I mean, how would you feel about … Erm, I wondered if … how about us getting married?' At last, after much stuttering, I got the crucial word out.

'Yes,' she said straight away. 'I'd love to.'

Chapter Twenty

Pat and I were married in July 1957 in St Patrick's Church in Newport. Mam and my stepdad, Betty and Rose and their families came to the wedding. We found a small flat near the rugby ground to set up home and for a while I felt like the luckiest man on earth – but it wasn't long before the ghosts of my past crept back to drag me down again.

I still worked for Watts Tyres, but I was also contracted to the British Road Services and worked shifts, going out on location to change the tyres of any truck that got a puncture within a twenty-mile radius. It was all right in summer, but in winter it could be cold, lonely, dangerous work. Sometimes the tyre-fitting had to be done by the edge of a road of fast-moving traffic and I'd heard horror stories about fitters being sucked under passing lorries.

Our first child, a little girl we called Maria, was born in May 1958, and it was a major learning curve for me. I'd spent my entire life in an all-male environment and I suddenly had to learn basic things, such as how to steril- ize a bottle, how to wind a baby after a feed, and even how to make a meal if Pat was tied up. Often I was exhausted if I'd been out on shift the night before, and the old depression began to creep up on me.

I had a chip on my shoulder about my under-privileged background and lack of education, and my temper would rise quickly if I felt anyone was criticizing me. I was very conscientious, often working extra hours without claim- ing overtime, but I'd become aggrieved if I didn't feel my efforts were appreciated. At the least little disagreement, I would tell my boss to 'Stuff it!' and walk out. Mr Alford knew my history and bent over backwards to help me but eventually I'd had enough and left Watts Tyres. Fortu- nately I had enough contacts in the tyre trade to walk into a new job fairly quickly, but I wasn't doing myself any favours. I spoiled several good career opportunities because if I felt things weren't going my way I would make sure I rejected the potential employer before he could reject me. I couldn't bear anyone to have power over me.

After a long day at work, I frequently felt I needed to unwind before going home, so I took to going to the pub with my workmates for a few pints and a game of cards or darts. Of course, Pat got annoyed at this, because she had been on her own with the baby all day and would have my dinner ready on the table, so we rowed, and as a result I'd spend even longer in the pub. I couldn't cope with quarrelling, even just the normal kind of domestic argument that all couples have. I'd get disproportionately upset at the slightest criticism and storm out.

The truth is, it was hard for me to adjust to ordinary, everyday family life. All those years of being uprooted and moved from place to place, from foster parents back to institutional homes, began to take their toll and a restlessness took hold of me. Along with this came periods of deep depression, especially around Christmas and the anniversary of Dennis's death on 9 January. Old memories resurfaced and with these memories came anger. The only way I knew how to deal with the disturbing emotions was to drown them in booze, so that's what I did.

When our second daughter Julie was born on 9 January 1960 I was pleased, but at the same time worried that there might be some significance to her birth date. Was it a bad omen? I wrestled with my negative thoughts, and spent more and more time in the pub looking for my own version of anaesthesia.

The drinking soon started to catch up with me. One night I was driving home from the pub in a light pick-up truck with a heavy built-up wheel in the back. I cornered too quickly, the wheel slewed to one side and its weight turned the pick-up over. I bashed my head on the windscreen and was knocked out cold. I came round within a couple of minutes and, with the help of some passers-by, managed to push the van upright again, but this wasn't the last accident I would have. Soon after, I was driving home after closing time when I came upon a place where road works were being carried out and barriers surrounded a deep hole in the road. I braked too late, hit the barriers and the van careered down into the bottom of the hole. I managed to climb out unharmed, but someone watching on the pavement called the police and I was arrested and taken to the main police station.

Of course, when they took blood and urine samples from me, I was well over the legal alcohol limit. I didn't argue with them – it was a fair cop. The police were very good to me, and spoke in my defence in court, saying that the roads had been wet that night, but I was found guilty of driving over the limit. I was fined thirty pounds and lost my licence for twelve months. This meant I also lost my job.

You'd expect that any normal wife would rant and rave at her husband after an incident like this, but Pat didn't do that. Instead, she asked me if I would talk to a medical specialist about my mood swings and depression, and ask his advice about my drinking as well. I felt I could hardly refuse given the circumstances, so I went along for an appointment, all ready to be defensive if I felt the specialist was having a go at me. Instead, he turned out to be a kind, very understanding man, who explained to me that

I was suffering from depression as a result of the treatment I'd received in my childhood – not just the six months at the Goughs', but the frequent uprooting and my bad experiences in care. He said many people never recover from such backgrounds and end up in prison or as alcoholics or drug addicts living on the street, so I was doing well to have got so far on my own. He gave me some tranquillizers to help me relax and we had a couple of counselling sessions, but to be honest, I didn't feel he got to the root of the problem.

Part of my difficulty lay in the fact that I couldn't bear it when memories resurfaced. Minor triggers could set me off and I'd over-react and get terribly upset. The specialist had suggested that I should try to take some of those memories out of the box in my head and face up to them, so that I could put them into perspective as an adult and try to move on. I could sort of see what he meant, but I was scared as well, and not sure how to go about it.

As a first step, I decided to try and get in touch with Freddie and wrote to Shrewsbury local authority asking them to forward a letter. A few weeks later, a reply came from Freddie, saying he had now settled in Lancashire where he was working as a teacher under the name Fred Pickering. We wrote to each other for a while, just about our jobs and families, and in 1968 he told me that he and his wife were renting a house in North Wales for a two-week holiday and invited us to join them.

I had my driving licence back by this time and we drove up overnight through the Welsh Mountains to Colwyn Bay. Freddie had dark hair, whereas he had been fair when I last saw him, but otherwise I recognized his features, and I was so pleased to see him that we just hugged for ages. We spent a lot of time together on that holiday, going out for walks and talking about everything that had happened to us since we were parted in 1944, but also sharing memories of Dennis. He had known Dennis better than anyone else in the world apart from me, and it made me happy to remember some of the good times we'd all had together, playing in the fields at the Connops', or messing around in the pond during the summer of 1944 when Dennis and I were at the Goughs' and Freddie was at Mrs Pickering's. He had turned into a decent, well-educated man with an even temper, who had taken the Pickerings' name because he felt so settled with them. In his case, the foster parent arrangement really worked out. I couldn't help thinking that if things had gone the other way and I had stayed at the Pickerings' with him, I could have been a lot happier than I was. I definitely got the short straw. But then poor Dennis's straw had been even shorter than mine.

In the winter of 1965/66 there were a number of cases reported in the newspapers of children who had suffered cruelty while in local authority care and they really affected me, adding to my normal seasonal depression till on some days I was paralysed with grief. The *Sunday Mirror* started a campaign about the failings of the social services and they ran an article about Dennis. They said that had he lived he would have been thirty-three years of age, but that he had never been given a chance. He had been 'shockingly and brutally ill-treated in a lonely Shropshire farmhouse' after he was placed in the care of the local authority. It continued: 'The sufferings of the O'Neill brothers as exposed by the courts and the national press so shocked the British people that the government was forced to open an investigation. The result was a new law promising greater protection for boys like Dennis. Now the nation has again had its conscience stirred about the sufferings of a child in care [a little boy in Dorset who had been tortured while in foster care] and it may well be that the law should be changed again.'

When I read the article, I was so moved by it that I decided to write to the newspaper. 'Dear Sir,' I wrote, 'I am very shaken to see the name of my dead brother, Dennis O'Neill, in your article … but I am also very glad that you used the dreadful circumstances of his death, and the sadistic treatment we both received at the hands of our foster parents, to serve as an example that the things that were never supposed to happen again continue to do so.' I put my support behind their campaign and thanked them for highlighting the issues as they were doing: 'When I read of a campaign such as yours … I feel perhaps that my brother did not die a lonely, painful death for nothing.'

It was a gut reaction to the article rather than a thought-through action and I was surprised when, a few days later, I was visited by a *Sunday Mirror* reporter, asking if she could talk to me about my experiences. I couldn't think of any reason not to talk to her, so I invited her in and answered all her questions as truthfully as I could.

The following Sunday, on 13 February 1966, the newspaper ran a full-page story based on this interview, under the headline 'HAUNTED BY THE BRUTAL DEATH OF HIS BROTHER IN THEIR FOSTER HOME'. The journalist reported everything I had told her accurately, but the tone of the article sounded quite critical of my birth family and I think some of them were annoyed about that. It quoted me as saying that they were strangers to me and 'my mother is an acquaintance … The only family I have now is my wife and children.' I went on to say that the biggest thing I lost through all the thirteen years of upheaval in council care was my education. Also, I added, 'Institutional life definitely has a dampening effect and some children become, as I did, so subdued that they are shy and have great difficulty getting along with other people.'

The article discussed the Monckton inquiry that followed the Goughs' trial and noted that there had only been one cursory visit to the farm to check up on Dennis and me during the six months we spent there, and that it had been by an unqualified officer. It finished by saying that it was probably only the local doctor's refusal to sign a death certificate for Dennis that had saved my life. If his death had been put down to natural causes, I would have stayed with the Goughs and would almost certainly have perished myself. I remembered Mr Bolton talking about how close to death I had been when the police took me away and I shivered.

I was upset to hear from some members of my birth family that they weren't happy about the *Sunday Mirror* article, partly because they thought it was disrespectful to Mam, and partly because not all the younger members of the family had been told about my childhood and their deceased uncle. Their reactions made me angry as well as sad, though. It wasn't them who had had to live on Bank Farm. Dennis hadn't died in agony in bed beside them. I felt I had a right to tell my story if and when I felt like it.

It was winter-time and my seasonal depression was in full swing. My worst moods could be triggered by any number of things: a minor quarrel with someone; any feeling of being criticized; and snowy weather, which always took me back to the last few days at the Goughs. My health wasn't good, and I started to experience regular vomiting spells, particularly in the mornings. I'm sure it was stress-related, but it meant I was always starting the day on a sour note.

On the surface, my life appeared settled: I'd moved jobs several times but always found the next one without too much of a gap in between, and Pat had a good job working for the civil service. We'd managed to buy our own house and the girls were settled in a decent comprehensive school, but still the old restlessness haunted me, and still I drank too much to quell the worst of my moods. If Pat tried to talk to me about it, I would respond by storming out of the house.

In 1967, our eldest daughter, Maria, turned nine, the age I had been when I lived at the Goughs', and I shuddered to think of her ever being in similar circumstances. She was still so young and needy of us that I couldn't imagine how she would manage without us – or certainly without Pat. Had I been as naïve and dependent at that age? No wonder I hadn't been able to stand up to the Goughs, or tell a teacher at school about what was going on. Watching my small daughter, I began to understand more fully why I had stuck with the status quo and tried to work harder to please the Goughs, hoping that if I could just make them happy then everything would be all right. Children that age want to stick with what they know, no matter how bad it gets, because they're afraid of change.

All the echoes in my head were getting louder, and I frequently had visits in my dreams from the ghost I called Charlie. I'd waken in the morning confused and disturbed, as if there was something I had to remember that I couldn't quite put my finger on. Pat said that sometimes I shouted out in my sleep. I pondered on what the counsellor had said about facing up to my past and finally, after a lot of thought, I decided that I had to go back to Bank Farm and confront my memories there. It might be traumatic at the time but I hoped that, if he was right, it would bring some relief later.

Pat wasn't at all sure about the idea but she agreed that we could drive up there one weekend with Maria and Julie. We plotted our journey on the map and set off first thing in the morning, but as we crossed the Shropshire Hills and descended towards Hope Valley, we drove into heavy fog. It started off as a veil of mist but by the time we got near the village of Hope, we could hardly see six feet in front of us. I'd been getting more and more tense as we drew closer and I began to feel claustrophobic as the fog closed in. My chest felt tight, making it hard to breathe, hard to think clearly.

I pulled up and parked outside the village shop. 'That's where Dennis and I used to sell crab apples,' I said, my voice croaky. 'And over there is my old school.' I realized my hands were shaking and clasped them together in my lap.

I pointed in the direction of the school, but it was shrouded so completely in fog that we couldn't even make out the outline of the building. The car's headlights created white channels through the murk without making the view any clearer.

'I don't like it here,' Julie began to cry. 'I want to go home.'

Pat turned to comfort her, while saying to me, 'I'm not sure we'll be able to see much today. Maybe it's not such a good idea after all.'

'We've come all this way,' I argued, but inside I felt relieved to be given a way out. The atmosphere was too creepy. I didn't feel in the right frame of mind for it. The time wasn't right.

'Let's come back another day,' Pat suggested, and I turned the car around without any further prompting. As soon as we climbed out of Hope Valley the fog cleared and it was a bright sunny day again. I took that as a sign that I hadn't been meant to visit the farm that day. I put it to the back of my mind as something I would do in the future. There was no hurry.

In 1972 my brother Tom came up to Cardiff University to study for some further qualifications in childcare, and he and I began to meet and talk with each other. At one such meeting, I told him about trying to visit Bank Farm and about the fog that had descended, making it impossible to complete the trip.

'Why not try again?' he suggested. 'I'll come with you this time. It sounds as though it would be a good way for you to lay some of the ghosts to rest and I'd be interested to see it.'

I felt my stomach twist with nerves at the thought, but the more I considered it, the more I decided it might be a good thing to do.

We picked a day and, as luck would have it, the weather was once again bleak and miserable. Undaunted, we drove north, over the Shropshire Hills and down into Hope Valley. Visibility was better this time and I was able to show Tom the pond in the churchyard where we had splashed around in the summer of 1944, before we turned onto the long track up to the farm. It seemed even longer than I remembered it and full of potholes that made the car leap and judder. We parked the car at the top and got out to walk up to the farmyard. My heart was fluttering with every step. Tom was chatting away but I was so nervous I couldn't focus on his words.

The farmer came over to meet us and Tom explained who I was. 'Do you think we might have a look around?' he asked.

The farmer called out to one of his workers, who emerged from a barn.

'Terry?' the worker called to me. 'Terry O'Neill? How on earth are you? Fancy seeing you back here.'

It seemed he remembered me from school, although I have to say I had no recollection of him. This broke the ice, though, and the farmer agreed we could have a look around the yard and inside the house as well.

I walked carefully, as if the ghost of Mr or Mrs Gough might burst out at any moment. There was the chicken shed, the stables and the cowshed, just as they had been when Dennis and I slaved in there, feeding the animals and cleaning up after them. There was the spinney where we went rabbiting with Bob Smith. The farmer opened the kitchen door and I felt a bit faint as I stepped inside. There was the pantry where we used to try to steal the odd morsel of food. There was the big fireplace and beside it the cubby-hole where I had been locked one afternoon. There had been some alterations to the layout, and it had all been redecorated so it looked like a pleasant family room, but for me the atmosphere was stifling and I couldn't wait to get back into the fresh air again.

'Don't you want to see upstairs?' the farmer asked me.

'No, thanks, not today,' I said quickly as I turned for the door.

'Let's go!' I whispered to Tom, already heading back towards the car.

Tom called our thanks to the farmer and then caught up with me. 'You OK?' he asked. 'Your voice went all husky when we were in there and you kept coughing.'

'I felt as though I was choking.' My throat still felt tight as we climbed into the car.

'Let's go for a pint,' Tom suggested.

We stopped at a nearby pub, the More Arms, and as soon as I walked up to the bar, the publican recognized me.

'Terry!' he cried with a big grin. 'It's Peter. How are you doing? What brings you back here?'

He was another boy who recognized me from Hope village school, but this time I recognized him as well. We got chatting and he told us that his mother had bought

Bank Farm some years ago and he lived there for a time, but that strange things were always happening. They chained up the cows every night, but next morning one of them would always be unchained, and its chain would be lying on the barn floor. There were several other inexplicable occurrences that made them feel the farm might be haunted and he was relieved when they finally sold up and moved on.

He mused: 'The funny thing is that before it all happened, Mr Gough was quite well liked in this area. She wasn't – she was a bit stuck up and unfriendly – but he was all right. No one could believe what they did to you and Dennis.'

There was a question that had been burning in the back of my head and at last I had to ask it. 'Do you have any idea what happened to them after they got out of jail?'

'Mr Gough had to sell the farm, as you probably know. It all went to auction. When he came out of jail, I heard he took to sleeping rough. I never saw him but I was told he was sleeping for a while in a little brick shelter in the hills that shepherds used back in the old days. I'm pretty sure he's dead now. Certainly nothing has been heard of him for a long while.'

'What about her?'

'I don't rightly know, but she wasn't from around here. She'd moved here with him, so maybe she went back to wherever she came from. We always thought they got it wrong at the trial and that she was the stronger one of the two and more responsible for the evil than she let on. But who knows what happens within a marriage?'

I nodded. 'Thanks,' I said. It was enough for me to know that they weren't in the area any more and there was no danger of bumping into them.

Peter insisted that we ate a good meal on the house, and we sat in front of his blazing log fire reminiscing about friends we had known at school, and other happier memories from that time. When we left, I wasn't sure that I had completely laid my ghosts to rest but at least I had some happier memories of Hope to put in my memory box, alongside the awful, desperately sad ones of old.

Chapter Twenty-One

After the visit to Bank Farm, my curiosity was piqued and I decided to do some research into what had happened to Dennis and me there. I only had my own nine-year-old's memory of events, but I became curious to read about what came out during the Goughs' trial, and about the Monckton Inquiry that had followed it. I started taking my daughters down to our local library whenever I had a free hour or two and looking up old newspaper reports in their archives. At first the girls were happy to spend some time browsing through the books in the children's section, but I began to spend so many hours there that I know they got very bored and occasionally fractious.

Every day I discovered more about my past, and another piece of the jigsaw clicked into place. I hadn't even known the Goughs' Christian names – Reginald and

Esther – and it was strange seeing them written down, along with their ages – thirty-one and twenty-nine respectively. That was younger than I was by then.

I'd known roughly what killed Dennis but seeing it written in black and white in reports of the inquest was chilling: 'He died as a result of Acute Cardiac Failure, following violence applied to the front of the chest. Violence applied to the back by beating acted as a contributory factor. He was under-nourished, thin and wasted. He had septic ulcers on his feet and his legs were severely chapped.' I had to put the paper down at that point for the tears blurring my eyes – tears of self-pity as well as tears for Dennis.

At four stones, four and a half pounds, Dennis was roughly one and a half stones under the weight he should have been for his age. There were detailed descriptions of the marks – the cuts, bruises, ulceration and cracked skin patches – that covered his frail body. I felt sick and had to take several deep breaths as I read the paragraphs that detailed each of his wounds: their length, depth and severity.

How on earth could the Goughs have pled 'not guilty' with such a damning catalogue of injuries to account for? What sort of a case could they possibly have made in their defence? I'd had my suspicions at the trial, from the tone of the questions I was asked by their defence counsels, that they were trying to pin some of the blame on me, but I was in no way prepared for what I found out when I read the accounts of Mr Gough's testimony in court.

He claimed that Dennis and I killed two of his calves by deliberately beating them, first with a stick and then with a shovel. He said they lost nearly thirty chickens as a result of us kicking them. He considered calling the police and reporting us but decided against it. The night Dennis died, he said that after we'd all had dinner he had only tied Dennis to the pig bench to try to scare us by letting us know what the police would do to us if we were caught. He claimed he hadn't beaten him but that we ran away laughing and weren't scared at all.

I was seething with rage as I read the report, with pictures of that hellish night as vivid in my mind as if it were yesterday. Mr Gough continued that when we went up to bed that night, we were fighting incessantly. He said: 'Dennis had pushed Terry to the end of the bed, he was trying to push him out of bed, I had to pull him back twice … They were just as bad as each other … I told them that if they would be quiet I would get them a cup of tea and some bread and butter … but after that they resumed their falling out.'

I wanted to shout at the page. 'If Dennis had had dinner and then bread and butter later, as you say, how come the inquest doctor said his stomach was completely empty? You liar! You bloody liar!'

The next morning, Mr Gough said, I told them that Dennis had been swinging on a door and had fallen off.

He seemed in a bad way 'but we didn't know really whether he was bad or whether he was having a turn, like he had the week before, "play act business" as he called it.' Seemingly they told the court that Dennis was always 'pretending' to faint and then he'd jump up with a laugh and claim he was fine after all. He wasn't, of course. He fainted because he was malnourished. He collapsed because he was weak as a kitten. And the business about swinging on a door was complete invention. When I woke up that morning Dennis was either already dead or in a coma. I don't believe he ever regained consciousness that morning.

Mr Gough was shown some photographs of Dennis's injuries and he told the counsel that he could not account for them. As far as he was concerned, we had been fed four, sometimes five meals a day, including meat and fish, and he had never struck us apart from the occasional stripes on the hand with his stick. We were very naughty boys who were always fighting each other and causing trouble, and he treated us with nothing but kindness, dressing our chilblains with his own hands and seldom raising his voice.

How could he have stood there and said all that? I was almost exploding with rage. It became obvious to me that he didn't have a shred of remorse for what had happened. He felt hard done by: we had come to his farm and caused him all this trouble. That was his attitude. He even launched an appeal against his conviction in June 1945, but the judge threw it out of court within fifteen minutes, saying 'Even assuming they were irritating, annoying sorts of children … that can never be enough to justify a grown man in doing the horrible things which according to the evidence he did to this unfortunate child.'

Mrs Gough took a different position, claiming that she was always very fond of me. She said I once put my arms round her and kissed her goodnight, and I shuddered at the thought. Had it happened? I didn't think so. She said she was terrified of Mr Gough, who often knocked her about, and that she was too scared of him to defend us. In response to the counsel's question, she said that although her husband made Dennis stand by the table and miss meals, she tried to slip him some food while Mr Gough was out in the fields. It was a black lie, of course. She was the first to scream 'Theft!' when a morsel of food went missing from her pantry. She urged Mr Gough to punish Dennis for sucking milk from the cows' udders and taking a bite from that swede. And what about the day before Dennis died when Mr Gough was in Welshpool? Why didn't she attempt to feed him then? In his summing up, the judge rightly pointed out that all she had to do was take Dennis to a doctor and the truth of what was happening at the farm would have come out.

It seems that Mrs Gough had written a letter to Newport Council in late December, saying that she and her husband would like to keep me, as I was much brighter and stronger than Dennis, and looked as though, when I left school, I would be capable of doing something. However, Dennis was 'dishonest, and not even capable of washing himself' and 'if we got him a job we doubt he would hold it any longer than the first day'. I tried to think what could possibly have led them to believe that I was a better worker than Dennis, and I could only come up with the reason that they always expected much more of him because they thought he was older than he was. They believed he was thirteen when he died, whereas he was only twelve. Had that made the difference?

I read an article once about 'survivor guilt' and I suppose I suffered from that to an extent. Certainly, I questioned why I survived when Dennis didn't. And the only answer I ever came up with was that I was younger and so much smaller when we arrived at Bank Farm that I became Mrs Gough's favourite. I spent more time with her than Dennis did, while, as the eldest, he was expected to be out in the fields doing heavier work with Mr Gough. I survived the lack of food better than Dennis did because I was smaller and didn't need so much nutrition to keep me going. Dennis was never cheeky to the Goughs in the way that I might have been back in the beginning before I became terrified of them. He was polite and respectful and didn't put a foot wrong. It's just that he was older than me. That's why he died.

The judge's final summing up was very moving: 'This child died miserably,' he said, 'with ulcerated sores and a condition such as the poor body so reduced could not withstand. All that happened not in a slum, not in a hovel, but in a farm on our countryside, on a farm where milking cows were kept, and where there were two people, a man and his wife, receiving payments of about two pounds [a week] for looking after them. Within half a mile was a school; somewhere near was a doctor. Apparently shops were not far away. There was a district nurse; there was a telephone. No wonder public opinion is stirred by this.' Then there was the passage Mr Bolton had told me about before, where the judge told the jury how honest my testimony had sounded.

I remembered that judge, Mr Justice Wrottesley, who had made me nervous at the time because he seemed so grand, but who had treated me with utter kindness. It's people like him who give you faith in the British legal system.

Occasionally, after long hours at the library, I came home and told Pat what I had found out. But most of the time I retreated into my shell and became bad-tempered with her and the children, or I went to the pub and drowned my sorrows. Certain areas were just too hard to bear and voices in my head said 'Have a drink now, you deserve one. You need it.' I can't have been much fun to live with. It was like peeling away layers of skin and exposing the painful, raw bits all over again, but once I'd started I had to see it through until I had read every document I could possibly find.

There were some revelations in the news reports that astonished me. In particular, I read that the water supply at Bank Farm flowed through an old lead mine. According to experts, the likely cause of the Goughs' chickens and calves dying was lead poisoning from the water they drank. I remembered the guilt I had felt when accused of killing them, and the amount of soul-searching Dennis and I did about whether their deaths could possibly have been our fault. All the time it was the water! No one had ever told me that. I felt a fresh wave of anger.

And then I came upon the testimony of Miss Edwards, the social worker who had visited us on 20 December. She admitted that she hadn't been able to talk to either of us on our own that day; she admitted that she hadn't seen upstairs into our bedroom; but still she returned from that visit so alarmed that she wrote a report on the 22nd advising that Dennis and I should be removed from the Goughs' as a matter of urgency. Why hadn't it happened?

It seems a letter was written to Shropshire County Council on 30 December but it failed to convey the urgency that Miss Edwards wanted it to convey. The letter arrived on 4 January and was put aside to be dealt with by someone called Mr Davies, who only returned to work from the holidays on the 10th – the day after Dennis died. Miss Edwards must have been devastated when she heard the news. If she had called a doctor herself that day, chances are Dennis would still be alive. She was only a young woman at the time, but I could imagine how that knowledge must have weighed on her conscience afterwards.

There were so many 'if onlys'. I read that the social worker who came at the end of the summer of 1944 and took the Mullinder children away had said in his report that the Goughs' place 'wasn't fit for keeping rabbits in, never mind children'. Why did no one put two and two together and realize it wasn't fit for Dennis and me? The headmaster at our school had reported that the Goughs were not satisfactory foster parents, but no one seemed to have listened to him either.

All the near misses, the times we were almost saved, were frustrating, infuriating and dreadfully upsetting. How could it have happened? I decided to read the reports of the Monckton Inquiry that followed the Goughs' trial, to see if I could find out why the system let us down so badly. One reason it gave was that the local authorities were understaffed and overworked because it was wartime. Some staff members had signed up for the Forces and the duties of those who remained had been extended to include finding suitable homes for children evacuated from cities. In our case there had also been some tragic errors in the filing system that had meant we slipped through the net. Newport Council assumed that the Shropshire authorities were checking up on us, while Shropshire thought Newport was doing it. But still, it seems, the normal 'boarding out' rules had not been followed with regard to us.

Sir Walter Monckton recommended, among other things, that in future each child taken into care should have one person who followed their progress all the way through until they were finally in employment. In 1947, several of his recommendations were taken on board: from then on an official had to visit each foster child within a month of them arriving in a new home, and every six weeks thereafter. They were also to be registered with a doctor and checked out by him within a month of arrival and thereafter at least once a year. The Children's Act of 1948 stated that each local authority should have a children's committee responsible for finding suitable foster homes for children in care, and a children's officer to oversee their decisions.

Throughout the reporting, Dennis and I were mentioned constantly. We were famous. Of course, I would give anything for it not to have happened, but I felt quite proud that so many important people had been concerned about us and that an Act of Parliament had been passed because of us.

'Have you found out enough now?' Pat asked when I told her about it. 'Do you think we can start to move on?'

I narrowed my eyes. What did she mean 'we'? I tensed, all ready to start an argument with her. It was *my* past, *my* brother who had died, *my* name in all the old newspaper reports – not hers. I looked hard at her and I saw the anxiety in her expression, the tired look in her eyes, and I realized that she was living through all this as well.

So were the girls. I wasn't able to leave my emotions at the library or let them dissipate on the road home. I'd been coming back to our house full of all the rage and anguish that I'd suppressed for the past twenty-five years and it had been affecting my entire family. They'd had to live with it, just as I had.

'Yes, that's enough,' I agreed quietly.

Frankly, I couldn't have coped with any more. It was a relief to get back to worrying about everyday things like paying the bills, and how Maria and Julie were doing at school, and whether we should retile the bathroom or not. It was time to be Terry O'Neill, family man, and not the 'tragic victim of an evil couple on a lonely farm' any more. That was then. Thirty years on, it was time to start focusing on all the things I had to be thankful for. It was time to close the memory box, put it away and live in the present once more.

Epilogue

I think Pat would agree that I mellowed with age. The trickiest years of our marriage were in the 1960s and early 1970s, but as our daughters grew up, left home and made their own ways in life, I settled down a bit. I still had a restless streak that made me leave jobs every couple of years, but I found a channel for my energy in the early 1980s when I got involved in local politics and was proud to be elected a member of Newport town council from 1983 to 1986.

After I retired the past started to creep up on me again, but I found that I could think about it without the bitterness and fury I'd had before. It was sad, but so were a lot of other things in life. I still got my winter depressions but I knew how to sit quietly and wait until they passed. Maybe the emotions were easier to manage because I'd cut right back on my drinking. Maybe it was just the passage of time.

One thing still brought tears to my eyes, though, and that was reading news stories about other children who had been let down by the system and had died horrifying, painful deaths. In 1973, there was seven-year-old Maria Colwell, who was beaten to death by her stepfather despite neighbours making at least thirty calls to social services. In 1984, four-year-old Jasmine Beckford was starved and battered to death by her stepfather; he'd already been convicted for assaulting her younger sister, but Jasmine was seen by a social worker only once in the ten months before she died. In 1985, a five-year-old called Heidi Koseda died of starvation and was only found in a cupboard two months later; her mother and the mother's boyfriend were both jailed. It was partly as a result of these cases that I decided, in 1991, to start writing my memoirs. If I could do anything at all to prevent cases like these ever happening again, then I felt it was a worthwhile thing to do with my retirement.

I had no writing experience at all, so it was always going to be a laborious process. I wrote it by hand first, then typed it up on an old typewriter, then retyped it on to a Commodore computer. The cartridges the Commodore took were incompatible with my next PC, which I bought in 1999, so it was time for another retype, and somehow nineteen years passed since the day I started writing!

Pat was alarmed at first when I began my fresh journey into the past, but she was happy to accompany me on trips to flesh out the pictures I had stored in my memory of different parts of my life. In June 1994, we went to a reunion of former pupils at Croft Castle School, which I had attended when I stayed with the Connops. It was lovely to think back to that period when Dennis, Freddie and I had been happy and care-free. I marvelled at the length of the spooky drive we walked along twice a day to get to school, and managed to find the pond where the watercress grew. What's more, I got into conversation with a National Trust employee who was now living at the Connops' old house and she invited me back there for a look around at the big rooms and the oak-panelled hallway with the alcove where the lodger died.

Every August Bank Holiday, I go to a reunion of Blaisdon Hall old boys and I always feel great warmth towards them. They rescued me at a time when I was a taciturn, institutionalized, resentful young lad, and if it hadn't been for the kindness they showed me and the lessons I learned there, I could easily have followed the wrong path in life and ended up in jail, or as a destitute alcoholic. Through some friends I made at these reunions, a trail led back to the village of Hope and I got in touch with Gladys Hordley, whose brother Dennis had once stolen sandwiches from. She phoned me one day in July 2003 to say that she had been talking about me with the present owners of Bank Farm, and that we were invited to go back there for another visit if it would help with my research for the book.

I spoke to the owners, Frank and Myriam, on the phone and they sounded so warm and friendly that I had no reservations about making the journey this time. The fields were awash with golden sunlight and the hedgerows were overgrown with lush grass and wildflowers as I drove north towards Hope Valley once more. I turned onto the track that led to Bank Farm, dodging the potholes, and as soon as I pulled up in the yard, Myriam came out to greet me. She led me straight into the house, and I felt apprehensive but didn't like to say so.

The layout of the ground floor had been changed. We went in through the front door, then down a passageway to the kitchen. The fireplace with the cubby-hole was still there but the walls of the old pantry had been torn down and only the windows out to the yard remained. It was different, but it was the same as well. I could see the nails hammered into the wooden beams from which the Goughs' hurricane lamps used to hang. There was the spot in the corner where the pig bench was kept.

Suddenly, to my great embarrassment, I burst into noisy floods of tears. I was sixty-eight years old, and it was more than fifty-eight years since the night Dennis died, but it felt so immediate.

'Do you want to sit down?' Myriam asked, worried about me. 'Can I get you anything?'

I dried my eyes and blew my nose. 'No, I'd like to go upstairs, if that's all right with you.'

I'd forgotten that it was only a couple of short flights of four or five steps up to the room where Dennis and I slept. In my mind it had become more. Myriam opened the door and stood to one side to let me in and my first reaction was that I couldn't believe how small it was. To me, as a child, it had seemed much bigger – a large, cold, bare room. I explained where the straw mattress had been, the mattress that Dennis was dying in as he lay next to me. I started crying again as I described the events of that last night when my brother had clawed at my back in agony and there was nothing I could do to help him. I told her about wakening up in the morning and trying to rouse him, to no avail. I stayed in that room for some time, just looking and thinking, and it was as if Dennis was with me. I could feel his presence, but it was a calm feeling, as though things were settled now. He was at peace, and I could be at peace too.

Eventually, I continued the tour, looking at the bedrooms up the other staircase, where the Goughs had slept and the Mullinder children had been put in our place. These rooms were also much smaller than I remembered them. Finally, we went down to the lounge, which was a big room created in the area where the cowshed used to be. Myriam brought tea and I relaxed as I sat chatting to her. Pat and I had often used the phrase 'laying the ghosts to rest' and finally, by coming back to that bedroom, I felt I had actually done it. I'd faced up to the worst thing that had ever happened to me and found that it was bearable. Bitterly sad, yes – but bearable.

While I was writing this book, my brother Tom got in touch to say that his son Bernard had been at a conference when another delegate picked up on his surname – O'Neill – and asked if he had anything to do with Dennis O'Neill, the boy who had been killed at Bank Farm.

'Yes,' he replied. 'He would have been my uncle.'

'Did you ever see the Agatha Christie play *The Mousetrap*?' the man continued. 'Did you know she wrote it after hearing about the O'Neill case?'

'You're joking!' I shouted when I heard the news. Pat and I were big Agatha Christie fans, who loved watching *Poirot* and *Miss Marple* on the television. It seems she first of all wrote a radio play called *Three Blind Mice* in 1947, then she turned it into a short story, and finally she created the stage play known as *The Mousetrap*, which became the longest-running play in history, having been shown continuously in London's West End since 1952. I quickly got hold of a copy of the play text and read it from cover to cover.

Every audience is instructed not to give away the twist in the ending, but I am not breaking any rules by telling you that the plot is about me, as an adult, coming back to seek revenge for what happened in my childhood. As if I would do such a thing! I didn't mind at all that she had used my story. I was only sorry that Agatha Christie had died in 1976 or I would have written to thank her for putting me in one of her works.

While I've been writing my own story, I've become more aware of the effect my depressions and drinking must have had on my family over the years. Pat has been a saint to put up with me for so long and tells me that in the 1960s and 70s she sometimes thought I was on a mission to self-destruct. Alcohol brought all my suppressed anger to the surface and I would storm off at the slightest provocation – but somehow our marriage managed to survive, largely due to Pat's forgiving nature. I look back on my daughters' childhoods with special regret because I know I wasn't always the father I should have been. I decided to ask them both to write about what it had been like living with me, and the results were humbling.

Here's part of what Maria, my elder daughter said:

I know now with an 'adult head' why you didn't show us much affection, hugs and cuddles (as far as I can remember). It must have been difficult for you after the terrible childhood you'd had. I just know that I always loved you and was always seeking your approval … I never felt neglected or anything really awful when I was growing up, because we always had Mam who put us first, but she couldn't have had much of a life in those times.

When I had Laura and Adam, you were the perfect grandfather. You've always shown them love and attention and they adore you. You have been a reliable, steady, loving person they can turn to. Throughout my marriage problems, illness and divorce, the closeness between us grew. Mam always worried so much that I didn't want to add to it. Little did I realize that although you seemed calm, you went home and couldn't sleep for worrying yourself.

But all in all, we had a really good upbringing. We've all got our faults and with hindsight would do things differently, but we know we have a loving family.

In Julie's letter, she says:

I was always a very nervous child and, thinking back to our home life, I remember a tense atmosphere. Alcohol very often played a part and I was always waiting for you to come home from the pub. Whenever we planned a day out, we would be left waiting by you until, by the time you came home, it would be too late or not worth going any more. You seemed distant and moody and I remember you being particularly anxious around Christmas time. For several weeks before and after Christmas you would be sad and quiet and I felt for some reason that I was to blame, although I was never really sure why. It wasn't until I was older that I found out that my birthday and the anniversary of Dennis's death were on the same day – the ninth of January. I can see now it must have been a very sad reminder for you.

I was extremely moved by these letters and the love and forgiveness with which my girls wrote them. I'm a lucky man to have such a close family after all I've put them through, and nowadays I'm careful to let them know how grateful I am. I've got through the worst of my depressions, and if one comes along I can recognize the warning signs and take myself off somewhere quiet to reflect rather than heading straight for the pub.

The only thing that still affects me badly is press reports about children who have 'slipped through the net': poor little Victoria Climbié, who was starved, beaten and trussed in a bin bag by her great-aunt and the woman's boyfriend in 2000; Ainlee Walker, who died of sixty-four separate injuries received at the hands of her parents in 2002; and then the shocking case of Baby Peter in 2008, a boy still too young to talk, so he had no chance of telling anyone what was going on.

I look at my three grandchildren – two girls and a boy – and my two great-grandchildren – a girl and a boy – all of them bright and healthy and loved, and I know how lucky I am. It took me many long years to find a happy family life but at last I have one now, and I hope I still have a good few years left in me to enjoy it.